KATIE V PETER

THE INSIDE STORY OF THEIR DIVORCE

KATIE V PETER

THE INSIDE STORY OF THEIR DIVORCE

EMILY
HERBERT

JOHN BLAKE

Published by John Blake Publishing Ltd,
3 Bramber Court, 2 Bramber Road,
London W14 9PB, England

www.johnblakepublishing.co.uk

First published in paperback in 2010

ISBN: 978 1 84454 927 6

British Library Cataloguing-in-Publication Data:

A catalogue record for this book is available from the British Library.

Design by www.envydesign.co.uk

Printed in Great Britain by CPI Bookmarque, Croydon, CR0 4TD

3 5 7 9 10 8 6 4 2

Papers used by John Blake Publishing are natural, recyclable
products made from wood grown in sustainable forests.
The manufacturing processes conform to the environmental
regulations of the country of origin.

Contents

CHAPTER ONE

End of a Dream

The end, when it came, was brutal. On 8 September 2009, at the High Court in London, divorce proceedings were under way. District Judge Bradley was working his way through a list of 21: second to last were the names of a couple who were cross-petitioning each other for a divorce on the grounds of unreasonable behaviour, under the names Price K v Andrea PJ – Peter Andre's real name.

The names were read out, Judge Bradley pronounced decree nisi and said that the papers involved would not be made public as Peter's lawyers had made an application to keep them private until a full hearing into whether they should

be made public. The whole proceedings took just over a minute: Katie Price and Peter Andre were divorced. Their marriage had lasted just three years.

And so it was over for Britain's most famous couple. But just what had gone wrong? After Pete's shock decision to walk out on Katie the previous May, the couple had been increasingly at loggerheads, but matters escalated in previous weeks. Any chance that the duo might have had of keeping matters civilised had evaporated months previously, with a fierce war of words from the outset. All sorts of rumours swirled around as to the cause of the split and these were to intensify over the coming months as the two fought a public-relations battle to win the greatest support and neither seemed inclined to keep things amicable. In her hurt and rage, Katie lashed out at Pete and, while he attempted to keep cool, often he was provoked beyond endurance and so, in turn, lashed out himself. Matters did not improve when, over time, Katie was to form another relationship, while her ex-boyfriend Dwight Yorke also got roped into the mix. At times, it seemed, this was war.

The first really public battle was about who had been unfaithful to whom, although, if truth be told, it was probably neither of them. The marriage fell apart for very different reasons, but both had admitted to

being jealous where the other was concerned, Katie had allowed herself to be photographed with other men and anyway, no one could quite believe that two such sought-after people would split up without anyone else being involved.

Pete, in particular, was incensed by any accusation that he had cheated on his famous wife. Back in early June, shortly after the decision to split was announced, he was adamant that he had been a good husband from the start. 'I never once strayed from Kate,' he told friends. 'I was brought up to believe marriage was for life and this goes against everything my family and I stand for. Kate and I had our troubles like any other couple, but I never gave up until the very, very end. I would never walk away from the marriage without thinking about it long and hard; I didn't just up and fly the nest. I believe marriage is for life and this has left me utterly devastated.'

It had, too, but then Katie was clearly badly affected as well. Right from the start, she put on a much tougher show than Peter, but a dramatic weight loss when she appeared on the Clothes Show Live in late May clearly illustrated that she was taking it much harder than she let on. Neither of them appeared able to talk to the other, however, with the result that both were clearly knocked for six about it all.

KATIE V PETER – THE DIVORCE

Katie continued to put a brave face on it, but her actions told a different story. She was partying hard, often causing chaos wherever she turned up. The reality was that she was indulging in extreme behaviour to try to forget all her troubles, but, still, it didn't look good. A case in point was a Boyzone concert at Wembley Arena, during which she seemed totally out of control.

'Jordan was an absolute car crash – it was really sad and quite disturbing to see her in that state,' said one observer. 'She had been drinking before and during the show. Then, when it got to the big finale, where the band are raised up over the crowd on cables, she stumbled into the sound mixing table and spilled her drink all over it. The band's microphones cut out and the earpieces they wear to receive instructions from the show director started malfunctioning and making a really high-pitched screeching noise in their ears.

'They had to pull them out – it was an absolute disaster, but Jordan carried on laughing and dancing around with her mates. Many of the fans in that area could clearly see what she was getting up to and, by the end of the gig, there was more people pointing at her than at the band. They looked amazed that she was behaving like that in full view of so many

people. It was just sad to see her like that. She's clearly very emotional and taking the split very badly … It's a shame to see her like that.'

It was easy to mock, not least because Katie had spent much of her twenties falling out of nightclubs with a new man on her arm, but this time her behaviour seemed to signal a kind of desperation. When people are very hurt, they resort to extreme behaviour, including getting drunk in an effort to forget about their woes, and, clearly, this was what was happening here. Katie wasn't happy: she was having a horrible time and doing whatever she could to numb the pain.

Other people recognised that, too. Boyzone's Mikey Graham spoke for the rest of the band: 'We're obviously concerned for her and hope she gets through whatever troubles she has at the minute,' he said. 'We had no idea she was coming to the gig until she turned up just after it started.'

In many ways, it would have been better for her had she just admitted how hurt she felt and simply hid away, but that wasn't Katie – her style was to get out there and show she was fighting, which is exactly what she did. It was Pete who admitted he was finding it very hard; even though he had left her, rather than vice versa, the couple had been married,

5

after all, and had two children between them, Junior Savva Andreas and Princess Tiaamii Crystal Esther, as well as Katie's son with footballer Dwight Yorke, Harvey, whom Pete treated as his own. In fact, the children grew to be as much a focus for fighting as anything else, with everything from the amount of time Pete got to spend with them to the appropriateness of introducing them to their parents' new partners becoming a focal point of debate.

Pete, in particular, was emphatic that the children should not see their parents with other people while they were still legally married and was furious when his estranged wife soon began to take a different tack. He also continued to react angrily, when asked if he was seeing someone else. The answer was a firm 'no'.

'I can confirm the story in one magazine saying I'd grown close to three other women was total lies,' he said. 'Apparently, I've got one woman in Cyprus, another in Los Angeles and I'm involved with a member of staff. I can hold my head up high and say I've been 100 per cent faithful throughout my marriage, and still am. Any reports suggesting otherwise are hurtful and false.'

It was a stance he was to maintain, not least out of respect for his children, clearly concerned about the

trio seeing new partners move too quickly into their parents' lives.

Even at this early stage, several themes were beginning to emerge that would play out over and over again as the divorce began to roll through. The first was the PR battle between the two of them. Right from the start, Katie appeared out in public, over and over again, in ever-skimpier outfits, often drunk and, after not too long, with a man on her arm. Pete, on the other hand, was frequently seen with the children, taking them for days out and playing with them.

Gradually, the two began to be viewed as two totally different personas in the public eye: raunchy Katie and saintly Pete. This went beyond just how she appeared in the papers, though, as far as Katie was concerned: since meeting Pete, and especially since marrying him, she had transformed her public image from a glamour girl to a role model. A lot of her fans now were young girls, who bought her horse books, and whose mothers would be not be too pleased to see her leading an increasingly wild lifestyle. Soon, Katie's advisers began to worry that the split would do her commercial harm.

Katie herself had also become concerned about it, albeit somewhat belatedly. She also began to display signs that she was a long way from being over Pete:

having point-blank refused to see him, possibly as a tactic to make him see what he was missing, now she was reverting to the other extreme.

'For weeks, Katie was being a complete cow to Pete, insisting he deal with her through her mother, Amy,' said a friend. 'Katie moaned that she relaunched Peter's career when they got together – and now he is getting all the attention. She is worried fewer people are signing up for her internet fanclub – and thinks their fans have sided with Pete.' In actual fact, it was a close-cut thing: fascination for Katie remained as strong as ever, but Pete was certainly getting the better press.

But the other theme that was emerging and would continue to do so, even after the divorce, was that Katie wanted Pete back. She might have been putting on a very brave face in public but it was he, totally exasperated by their rows, who was the one who walked out and finally decided to put an end to the marriage. Peter Andre, unlike some of Katie's previous boyfriends, is a kind and thoughtful man, and, as is so often the case, Katie only realised what she'd lost when it was too late.

Pete was veering between anger and concern. On the one hand, he had to put up with his estranged wife being seen partying all over town, but on the other he could tell Katie was going off the rails, especially after one rather fun night out with Michelle Heaton. In private, too, Katie was urging him to reconsider, not realising that it really was too late.

'He knew she would be upset but thought their marriage had run its natural course,' said a friend. 'He feels really bad about the whole situation as he cares for Katie deeply and hates to see her like this. All her desperate phone calls are really heartbreaking, but he's determined to stay strong. Deep down, he knows that it's not right to get back together, no matter how much it's hurting Katie. In the long term, it's better for both of them.'

And then, again, there were the children: Pete was an avowed family man and hated being away from them so much, on top of which there was the situation with Harvey. Pete might not have been his biological dad, but he was a father to him in every other way, and access was a grey area. 'Kate and I have three beautiful children,' said Pete, at one point. 'And so, for them, I want to keep things as amicable as possible. I love spending time with the kids – I would see them 24/7 if I could, so I don't want to get into a public slanging match with Kate. I just want us to be good parents.'

And, as if all that were not enough, both he and

Katie were seeing their weight plummet. It was a very uneasy state of affairs.

At least they both had their work. In June, Pete flew to Macau, China, to perform at the International Indian Film Academy Awards (IIFA) and this helped to cheer him up. 'The past four weeks have been the worst of my life,' he told a reporter. 'It was hell. No matter what happens, you never stop loving someone. Initially, I couldn't even have thought about work – my head was everywhere. It still is everywhere. But it's been a month now and I know I've got to start pulling myself together. The response I've had since being in China has been absolutely amazing. This, and the work I am doing now, is beginning to give me confidence again. Singing has given me something to focus on. I never expected the attention I've been getting and I am so glad this is happening. I've only been here a couple of days but it's already turned out better than I ever hoped. Finally, I am beginning to smile again. It's not like I'm a bundle of joy now, but it's getting better. I'm even cracking terrible jokes!'

He further revealed that the pair had tried marriage counselling although that, too, hadn't worked. Despite the shock caused when he walked out, the marriage had been in trouble for some time, and now it was far too late to try to piece it together again. 'Yes, it was Pete who left Katie – but not [until] after he had done everything in his power to make the marriage work,' said a friend of Katie. 'Neither of them take divorce lightly and both wanted their relationship to work for the sake of the kids, if nothing else. So Pete persuaded Kate to give counselling a go once they started having frequent, more hostile rows. He really was willing to try anything, if it might help. Although they both went into it willingly, it was more of a Band-Aid gesture – a desperate final attempt to patch up the marriage and make it work. Pete was devastated that it wasn't the solution.'

In truth, it was too little, too late.

Still, work continued to be a solace. Katie let it be known that she wanted to compete in the dressage and show-jumping categories in the 2012 Olympics, although how realistic that ambition was it was difficult to say. Behind the scenes, however, despite Pete's wish to keep matters pleasant for the sake of the children, bitterness was growing. One of the many reasons given for the break-up of the marriage was Katie's friendship with her married riding teacher Andrew Gould coupled with Pete's jealousy, but Kate and Andrew were adamant that they were just good friends.

It was, however, her friendship with Andrew that had been a big factor in Pete walking out. A couple of weeks before the split, Katie had gone for a big night out with some of the horsey set, with whom she was socialising increasingly frequently, (another factor in the problems between Pete and herself), and was pictured laughing and enjoying herself. Gould was also in the group, which many people believed was the final straw as far as Pete was concerned.

Gould attempted to defuse the situation. 'Kate, and I, and all her friends, have always socialised at shows and horse events,' he said, when it became apparent that his name was about to be made public. 'It was all harmless stuff and it has been blown out of proportion. We were just out socialising with friends, as we normally would. I don't see it's going to change. She's obviously quite distressed about what's going on. It's a time [when] she needs to be alone with her family, so I will respect that. I would say Peter is jealous because we have a close link – as far as horses go. It's just a horse thing.'

But it was also a sign that the two were growing apart. Pete made no bones about the fact that he was jealous where Katie was concerned, but this was more evidence that the couple were now moving in very different circles and they simply didn't fit together any more. But this made them both angry and, inevitably, it also made them lash out.

Katie seemed to veer between grief and fury. Indeed, the depth of animosity was revealed by Sol Gilbert, a fitness instructor and friend who was helping her to build up her physique. 'I'm not going to waste one more second on trying to get him back,' Kate told him, and added, 'I feel utterly humiliated – I'm getting caned every day in the papers. Usually stories like this die down, but this keeps on going every day – it's getting bigger and bigger.'

And it was: public fascination with the two showed no signs of abating. But what Katie couldn't understand was why the public seemed to be siding with Pete, and not her. Certainly, there was some feeling that she had pushed a basically decent man too far, but another problem was that Katie didn't seem to realise that the kind of behaviour that had made her a celebrity in the first place was seen by many as inappropriate now that she had three young children, while Pete, the doting father, was gaining all the public support.

As ever, she continued to fight back, working out to get herself into even better shape and she could always confide in her friends. Sol was also able to provide more detail on what had gone wrong. 'Pete rounded on Katie over her friendship with her riding instructor, Andrew Gould,' he revealed. 'It wasn't true [that she was having an affair], and Katie pleaded with him to believe her – but Pete wouldn't listen. She told me, "I begged him to stay to try to work things out for the sake of the children. I couldn't understand why someone would just want to walk out and leave their family."'

Clearly, she felt that the fact that she inhabited the world of the horsey set and Pete didn't had caused increasing tension between them. 'Pete didn't like the fact I enjoyed myself riding and would always come back with a smile on my face,' she told Sol. He would say, "Why are you so happy?" And he didn't like me going out socialising and having fun. Then he confronted me about my relationship with Andrew and I told him I just loved riding, but he didn't believe me.'

Of course, Katie was employing something of a selective memory here. In truth, the rows and tensions about any number of subjects had been simmering for months, but there was no doubt that she was absolutely shattered by what had gone on.

'I spoke to Katie when she was in the Maldives just after the split,' Sol continued. 'It was evening and I was at home and she was in her villa. She was devastated. She said, "I can't believe he walked out on me like that."'

The final, televised row between the two (broadcast in the UK in May 2009) had centred on fame: which was the better known of the two? Although this had not been the issue that had finally forced them apart, it did bring the couple's frequent rows out into the open. It was also one of the elements that had caused the public to feel very sympathetic towards Pete, but it was indicative of the kind of problems they had been experiencing and it certainly made for uncomfortable viewing.

The spat began when the duo were in a shop in the United States. Clearly, the shop assistant didn't have a clue about either of them, but the two started to squabble about which of them was the more famous and matters very quickly got out of hand.

'When someone knows who you are, and you come into a shop and you're blatantly lying, you look a twat,' Katie snarled, as the argument began to turn nasty.

'Really? Shhh, Kate, zip it!' returned Pete. He started speaking to the hapless shop assistant, who was looking as if he'd rather be anywhere but there. 'So, have you heard of Kate?' he asked.

'I'm not sure,' was his reply.

'How do you feel now?' demanded Pete, turning back to Katie. 'How do *you* feel?'

'You're a fucking knob, I can't stand you!' said his wife.

'Ahh, did I hurt your feelings?' asked Pete. 'Did he not know who you were?'

'Oh, as if I'm bothered,' responded Katie. 'No one knows who you are; you're an old fucking singer no one knows about!'

This was beginning to go too far.

'You've got a real attitude problem,' said Pete, who was looking furious.

'Get over it, Pete. I want to go home!' was her reply.

'I'm *so* glad you guys are here to film this,' said Pete to the film crew.

'I'm *so* glad too, so you know what a knob you are!' Katie replied.

'You can see what kind of a stupid, miserable, arrogant cow she is,' said Pete, and by this time it was becoming apparent that the row was really serious.

'Arrogant, what, 'cos I'm talking to someone genuinely and you're sitting there fucking lying? I can't stand liars!' Katie continued.

'*Really*? You've got fucking issues,' said Pete. 'I can't wait for you to watch this back and see how miserable you are.'

And now, alas, they finally got to the nub of it, which put Katie's next comments to Sol into context.

'*I'm* the one making money, Pete, so 'course I can have it how I want,' said Katie.

'What, don't *I* make money?' he demanded.

'I don't know, *do* you? Hurts, doesn't it?' Katie replied.

'How fucking dare you talk to me like that! Think you're gonna get away with it?' Pete retaliated.

At this point, the two were forced to shut up.

It was this row about money, the point being that the person who had the higher profile was the one who earned more, which brought matters to a head and so it was hardly surprising, in the months that followed, that this continued to be an issue. Pete was deeply upset when some voices within the media suggested the split was just a publicity stunt (although by now it was becoming apparent that it was anything but) and now Katie seemed to think that he was using the parting to get publicity for himself, too.

'Now I think he or his people are trying to exploit the situation for publicity,' she told Sol. 'He is trying to sensationalise it to launch his career. People don't see Pete for what he really is – he is more competitive than he comes across. Pete could never accept the fact I was the star: he was always going to be in my shadow and he just couldn't cope with it. He had a bit of success once, but he should have respected the fact that modelling as Jordan made the money.'

Perhaps it did, but no man wants to be made to feel second best. Maybe it wouldn't have mattered so much if Katie hadn't rubbed his nose in it, but Pete had been a star in his own right back in the 1990s, and no one likes to feel like a has-been. And, while Katie was probably the bigger celebrity by the time they got together, as a couple they had risen to dizzying heights of fame that they would never have achieved on their own. They worked best together, which made it all the sadder that they could no longer continue as they had before.

According to Sol, matters were now so bad between the two of them that they had only spoken once since Pete walked out. Katie was also extremely bitter about what she saw as her husband's attempts to relaunch his career.

'He was unemotional and Katie had to keep herself under control,' said Sol. 'She has told me, "Why is he moving to Brighton when he is trying to revive his pop career? Why isn't he moving to London? And, if it wasn't for what I did to relaunch his career, he'd be looking for a bedsit somewhere!" Katie feels Brighton is her area, and this is going to only make things harder for them both to move on.'

Of course, the seaside town was also where the children lived and so it made perfect sense for Pete to want to be near by, but Katie seemed unable to see that. Instead, the bitterness just got worse. According to many reports, in her heart she still wanted Pete back, but he simply refused to play ball. And so, as the realisation began to dawn that this really was the end, Katie just got harsher and harsher.

'I'm not going to hang on for him for one more second,' she told Sol. 'I want to get on with my career. I have tried and tried – I wish him luck with the future, but I'm moving forward now. I want to start working on the new calendar in a fortnight. I'm looking at beach locations in Spain and other countries around Europe. This time it's going to be 100 per cent natural, no airbrushing. I don't care if people ridicule me. This is how I make my living – and I don't have to apologise for who I am: it's what I've wanted to do for a long time. Pete has held me back and now I'm going to show him.'

Of course, Katie had not got to where she was without a certain degree of determination and now it really began to show. Determined to make a good public fist of her life, whatever she might be feeling privately, Katie organised a fourth birthday party for Junior, getting the children to dress up in fancy dress as their favourite cartoon characters.

'I'm so over Pete,' she told fellow guests. 'Today has been all about moving on with my life. It's been really hard, but I think I'm finally getting there. The party was all about me, my mates and the kids. Nothing else upsetting got in the way. It's a chance for me to let my hair down after a very sad few weeks; it's been the perfect medicine.'

There was a lot of speculation, however, as to how she was really coping and what was actually going on behind the scenes. But she certainly put on a good show at the party.

'Katie was having a whale of a time and didn't seem upset at all,' revealed one of the guests. 'She certainly wasn't acting like a woman going through a messy divorce. In fact, she was cracking jokes and laughing throughout the day as if she didn't have a care in the world.'

But that wasn't all. Katie (and, shortly afterwards, Pete) had just signed up for a new reality-TV show, a project which she felt would help her to break out from under the shadow of coupledom, to start to re-establish herself on her own.

'Peter doesn't know anything about Katie's deal,

which she helped engineer herself,' said a friend. 'She didn't want to be associated with Peter any more and ITV were more than happy to allow her a show of her own. Bosses want to schedule the shows at the same time, which will be interesting – especially which one gets the higher ratings!'

To say that Katie would want to trounce Peter is something of an understatement and this was an attitude that would only intensify as time wore on.

It seemed that nothing either of them did could be taken lightly any more. The day after Junior's party, Pete took the children off on holiday to Cyprus, apparently livid that the day had turned into something of a drinking session for Katie and her mates. Drink had often been another source of contention between the couple – he hated Katie going out and getting drunk, and, of course, she'd been doing that very publicly since the split. The fact that she was obviously drowning her sorrows didn't help much, either – whatever the reason, Pete disliked her getting out of control. And so another battle in the separation commenced and another argument reared its ugly head.

However, all that was as nothing compared to what was to follow. Pete and the children were off in Cyprus, leaving Katie free to do as she wished, and, while she might have felt the huge gap created by the absence of her estranged husband and the three children in her life, she wasn't one to mope around. It simply wasn't her style.

So, Pete had gone to Cyprus with the children. Well, let him! Katie, meanwhile, had plans of her own: she was going to spend a week in Ibiza with friends.

CHAPTER TWO

Ibiza Rocks!

Katie was ready to party. The initial shock of the break was behind her and now she needed to chill out, let her hair down and have a bit of fun. And so she set off for Ibiza, the biggest party island of them all, with a group of friends in tow. 'Yee haa, I'm going to have some fun at last,' she declared. 'It's been a fucking nightmare, but I'm going to have a wicked time. I haven't had a full week's holiday for ten years. I am up for it!' She was to prove as good as her word.

In typical Katie fashion, this was not just a holiday: she was combining the trip with a photo shoot for a new calendar. But she was intending to party, and party she did: very conspicuously, very overtly and, at times, in a manner so attention-seeking that she could hardly move for the surrounding press. The message was clear: Katie was back on the singles scene, totally over her husband and the world could make what they liked of her behaviour. And it did.

The party set off in mid-June on a 6.10am, easyJet flight from Gatwick, during which Katie had to endure the indignity of being frisked because her TV earpiece – the reality crew were following her every move – set off the detector alarm. Nor was she allowed to board the plane carrying a 150ml can of hairspray because it was over the 100ml limit. However, once on board, despite the early hour, everyone was clearly determined to enjoy themselves: the group swiftly got through four bottles of champagne, before Katie treated them to pictures of a naked man on her mobile.

'I hope I don't get into too much trouble,' she said gleefully. 'I'm determined to have fun. I've packed my slippers in case I have a quiet night in, but I doubt it.'

However, she managed to provoke yet more attention while studying an in-flight questionnaire, in particular, the question 'Are you pregnant?'

'Whoops, yes, I'm pregnant!' she said, before a spokesperson hastily reassured everyone that she was joking. And so they were off.

Not everyone was charmed, however. The cabin crew asked her if she'd pose for pictures with fans on board, but she declined. Nor was she in the mood to sign autographs. The airline staff became pretty fed up about it all. 'We can confirm Katie did fly with us to Ibiza – and also that unfortunately she was one of the grumpiest celebrities we've ever dealt with,' said an easyJet spokesperson. Katie herself let it rest.

As the repercussions of the break-up continued to spread, another element that would occur repeatedly throughout the months ahead was the steady stream of revelations about the couple, especially Katie's private life. Now was to be just such a case: it turned out that Katie had been on medication for much of her married life, but was now coming off it.

'I'm doing really well, focusing on the kids, my work, keeping fit and moving forward,' she commented. 'And, after four years, I'm no longer taking my anti-depressants. It has taken me four years to get to the healthy place I am now. I'm in a really good place.' Previously, her depression had not been widely known about, but one thing was clear: Katie wanted the rest of the world to know that it had been a problem throughout her relationship with Pete.

Once in situ, she headed for the Es Vive hotel where she was staying, one of the island's premier spots for partying (with a no-children policy), and donned a black bikini to relax by the pool. She and the rest of her gang ordered jugs of sangria. 'Katie feels absolutely drained,' said a friend. 'She's had an emotionally knackering five weeks and wants to let her hair down. Kate believes she works bloody hard for her money and deserves this trip. She's not got the kids with her, so she's not tied down. If she wants to go out every night and get hammered, then why shouldn't she? After all, she's a single lady now. Kate wants to treat all her mates and paint the town pink.'

However, it didn't all go according to plan. Katie clearly wanted to show her wild side again, but this didn't go down well with everyone: during the day she posed for pictures on Bora Bora beach, but one question was repeatedly heard from onlookers: 'Where's Pete?'

That evening, the party went to the Ibiza Rocks hotel to watch the Ting Tings. They then moved on to the Eden nightclub in San Antonio, where they added vodka, Jack Daniel's and more champagne, this time Veuve Clicquot, to the mix, having been

Breaking up is never easy – especially when there are children to consider. Katie and Peter adapt to the new regime of sharing time with their kids.

Above: A dejected Peter takes a break in Cyprus while coming to terms with the end of his marriage.

Below left: Stocking up on supplies for the kids.

Below right: Princess and Junior help Pete move in to his new home in Brighton.

Putting his marriage woes aside, Peter takes to the stage for a male strip show.

Katie's infamous trip to Ibiza.

This page, above: Relaxing with friends at a restaurant. *Below left*: On a shopping trip ahead of a big night out on the island. *Below right*: Out partying in a very memorable outfit.

Opposite page: It wasn't all fun, as Katie had her work cut out doing photo shoots for her calendar.

Katie gets on with life without Peter.

Above left: Making it clear she's looking after number one.

Above right: Peter's name scored through on Katie's arm.

Below left: A night out on the town with friend Michelle Heaton.

Below right: Even when you are as successful as Katie is, the kids need looking after and the shopping has to be done.

In June 2009, Peter attended the International Indian Film awards. He arrived with Bollywood actress Sophie Chaudhary and later performed for the audience.

Giving their respective sides of the story.

Above: Katie did a much-publicised interview with Piers Morgan, during which she broke down as she revealed how she and Peter had lost a baby shortly before their split.

Below: Peter on *Friday Night with Jonathan Ross*. This interview was less revealing than Katie's but the audience seemed to be firmly on his side.

given £300 'buckets' by the club. By this time, a clearly tired and emotional Katie started to gyrate up against a pole, before hooking up with male model Anthony Lowther, 28, who had arrived at the establishment dressed in tartan leggings, an outfit almost as eye-catching as the one Katie was wearing. The two were seen kissing – although Katie was also spotted kissing another man – and it was clear that they were getting on.

'There was chemistry between them,' said an onlooker. 'He was pouring booze into her mouth from the bottle, while she laughed and shrieked around. When she jumped on to the podium next to the DJ booth, she moved her body up and down seductively against his. Katie was acting as if her behaviour was totally normal; it was like she was putting on a show for everyone there. She was saying, "I can do this now, I'll be divorced in five and a half weeks!"'

Anthony picked Katie up and deposited her on a sofa at the back of the club, at which point her blue dress rose up over her head, exposing her G-string. Undeterred, she then started flashing her breasts. Finally, as the clock was heading for 5am, the two of them went back to the Es Vive hotel, while the others partied on.

Naturally, onlookers were deeply shocked. 'Katie could barely stand and kept putting her sailor's cap on people's heads in the queue,' said one. 'But when this pretty brunette went up to say hello, she just lost the plot.'

Katie had certainly got the eyes of the world upon her – although not, holidaying as he was in Cyprus with the children (and without the daily papers), Pete's.

The next day, there was more relaxing by the pool and more for the photo shoot, partly on the beach and partly back at the hotel, where other guests were irritated that they were banned from using the cameras on their phones. A speedboat ride followed, also for the calendar shoot, and Katie found time to update her Facebook entry, rather bizarrely threatening to shave off all her hair. But it was at night that she was coming into her own and so it proved again: that evening, the party was seen swigging sangria at Es Vive, before heading off for a three-hour dinner at Angelos restaurant. Once again, Anthony Lowther was present and happy to confirm that they were having fun.

'I'm having a great time with Katie,' he said. 'She's getting on with her life and enjoying herself without Pete. I know her from a few photo-shoot jobs I've done with her and we've always got on. She's having a blast and is enjoying being single again.'

The two were spotted taking a late-night walk around the harbour, before returning to the hotel. Friends, meanwhile, asserted that she had every right to behave as she pleased.

'Katie is back to her best, being Jordan,' said one. 'She doesn't care what people think, she's out to shock. She may be in the middle of an acrimonious divorce, but it's not getting her down. Instead, she joked she was horny and wanted to "get some" after a barren spell with Peter. Anthony picked up on the cue and was very attentive to her.'

The next day, the photo shoot moved to the nearby tranquil island of Formentera. Meanwhile, back in Britain, something of a backlash was beginning to develop. Every day, as pictures appeared of Katie behaving increasingly wildly, there were also shots of Pete, playing with the children in Cyprus. The contrast couldn't have been greater, and not everyone was on Katie's side – in fact, far from it. After all, technically, she and Pete were still married, and what about the kids? What would they make of photos of their mother so very publicly out on the razz?

What made matters even worse was that, while

Katie looked as if she was having the time of her life (although, in truth, her out-of-control behaviour almost certainly meant that she was still not dealing with her grief), Pete was so visibly upset. On arriving in Cyprus, he discovered that his mother Thea had flown to Larnaca from Australia with his sister Debbie to offer him moral support. Visibly moved, Pete wept on his mother's shoulder. 'He had no idea his mum was coming, so, when he went to collect his sister at the airport and saw Thea, it was all too much,' revealed a friend. 'The emotion of the past six weeks caught up with him, and, as much as he tried to hold it together, he simply couldn't. Thea will give him some much-needed TLC, and wants to look after him as only a mother can. She'll do him a world of good!'

Meanwhile, back in Ibiza, love's young dream was going through a sticky patch. Katie certainly wasn't about to clean up her act: there was another drinking session, this time Jack Daniel's and coke, as she informed startled holidaymakers, 'I am Katie Price now – demure, sophisticated and elegant. I am going to walk properly, but, after midnight, Jordan is coming out and you know what *that* means! Have some of that, you motherfuckers! I can drink what I like, and do what I like. Sorry, Mum!'

Demure wasn't quite the word for it: she flashed her dress at the camera crew before continuing to down some more shorts.

Katie was certainly as good as her word, however, when it came to turning into Jordan. A stream of bottles of Veuve Clicquot was seen being taken into her room, before she emerged at 10pm, already a little worse for wear. With her entourage in tow, she headed for Pacha nightclub, where she and Anthony danced between bouts of throwing back vodka lemonades. Katie was also seen kissing a strange girl, before she and Anthony headed back to the hotel, where they had one almighty row: 'I don't give a fuck any more!' yelled Katie, and at around 5.30am fellow guests complained to the hotel management about the racket coming from her bedroom. Hotel staff banged on her door in an effort to get the couple to keep the noise down, but this was all to no avail.

Unsurprisingly, shooting for the calendar was scrapped the next day while Katie slept it off. Now the cluckerati in the UK press were really beginning to have a go, with Pete being congratulated for walking out on a woman who seemed out of control; all the papers, meanwhile, were covered in shots of Katie with her head in the sand, bum held high.

When Katie did eventually surface, she didn't

make matters any better for herself, though. First, she visited Sa Majesté, a specialist gay and lesbian sex shop, where she bought a range of PVC outfits, whips and so on. Next stop was Inkadelic Salon, where she had the tattoo of Pete's name on her left wrist deleted with a cross.

'She looked like she was on a mission,' remarked an onlooker. 'I think it's fair to say she was trying to send out a message to Peter. She wants to leave him in no doubt that what they had is over. And there won't be any fairytale reconciliation; that's it now for her. Done and dusted!'

But it certainly didn't look as if things would last with Anthony. The row they'd had the previous night appeared to have shaken him, and now he was backing off fast.

'She's a gorgeous girl and I'm looking forward to spending more time with her,' he told a friend. 'But she's just getting over her split and she's been through so much, so I'm not expecting anything serious to happen yet. I'm not really up for getting involved in anything too heavy at the moment. I'm not ready to be a dad.'

That row, ironically enough, had been about Katie's totally OTT behaviour.

'Anthony is really softly spoken and actually has a

lot of mannerisms that would remind you of Pete,' said a friend. 'But Anthony and Katie fell out when he told her she was getting too lairy. He sees the good in everyone, but even he couldn't handle her on Thursday night.'

Meanwhile, back in Cyprus, Pete's family and friends were doing everything they could to protect him from what was going on, but there was only a certain amount of cover-up that they could manage, and, although Pete wouldn't see the full reports about Katie's behaviour in Ibiza, enough was getting through for him to be totally appalled.

'It's like a wild animal has been unleashed,' he told friends. 'I don't recognise her as my wife. Has she no idea what this will be like for the kids? It was Katie who I fell in love with and married, but it looks like she just wanted all along to be her old self, Jordan. I can't believe what I'm seeing – she's like a caged animal that's been let out.'

Among the people with Pete at the time was his friend Angelo, who became one of the first in his entourage to talk about what was going on. 'Peter cannot believe what he's witnessing,' he said. 'He is really, genuinely shocked. He's been very upset, but this morning he simply said to me, "I've shed my last tear for her. Kate is right about one thing: there were three of us in our marriage – me, Kate and Jordan." [a reference to an interview given by Katie the previous week].

'Katie has shattered his world – I can't keep quiet any more. I shouldn't be saying anything, but I'm absolutely livid and someone has to speak up in Pete's defence.'

In retrospect, the revelation of Katie's behaviour in Ibiza might well have had a lot to do with Pete finally being able to move on. With each passing day, he understood more clearly that the woman he married had a very wild side to her, that ultimately she could never have been the one for him. At the time, however, it was devastating and everyone around him continued to try to protect him as best they could.

'We dumped the papers in the bin to keep them from him because we knew it would break his heart,' said Angelo. 'But he found them and pulled them out. He couldn't believe she was cavorting with male models, wearing sexy clothes and looking like she didn't have a care in the world. Peter completely broke down.'

And it was certainly making him question the past. 'It's like my entire marriage has all been a sham,' Pete told his family. 'What is this going to be like for the children when they read how their mum behaves?

Maybe she never really was Katie, maybe Jordan was the real her with Katie the pretend person, rather than the other way round. It feels like she's been trying to force herself to live a life she didn't want to live. Seeing all those pictures of her topless, then drunk and falling about, just makes me want to weep.'

At least his mother was there to help. 'When Peter's mum arrived, it sparked all the pent-up emotion from the past few weeks and he couldn't stop crying,' revealed Angelo. 'It has killed me watching how sad Pete has been over the destruction of their marriage, but now he knows he has to move on.'

At least he still had the children to console him. A doting father and family man, Pete was delighted with the chance to spend time with the three of them, something that had been difficult since the separation.

'I can't even begin to tell you how happy it makes me,' he said at one point. 'Princess has become a total daddy's girl and I had a really beautiful moment last week on the beach that I'll honestly never forget. Harvey just put his arms round me and held me for what seemed like ages. Due to his condition, Harvey sometimes finds it hard to show his love, so that hug meant the world to me.'

Nor, at this stage at least, was he allowing himself to be drawn into a slanging match. 'Of course I still love Kate: if you get over someone in five weeks, then you obviously didn't love them in the first place,' he said.

Katie herself was beginning to realise her behaviour wasn't playing too well back home. She and Anthony hit the clubs once more, this time with Katie dressed in a very revealing gold lamé one-piece, but she was starting, very unusually, to sound a little subdued. There was, after all, a lot at stake: not just her career and her carefully revamped image as Katie, rather than Jordan, but also custody of the children to consider. This wasn't looking good.

'I've been acting like Jordan at her worst and Pete's destroyed me by acting like the perfect dad,' she glumly admitted. 'I know how it could play in the divorce court.'

Then there was the commercial aspect to it all. While Katie had made her name as Jordan, it was Katie Price who became massively popular, and who had signed up to all those lucrative sponsorship deals since coming out of the jungle, where she'd met Pete, five years previously. There were real fears that her erratic behaviour might bring all that to an end.

'Since coming out of the jungle in *I'm A Celebrity*, Katie has built a fantastically marketable career as Katie Price, mother of three children and a role model to young girls,' commented a marketing expert. 'In the space of five days, there is a perception she has seriously damaged that image. Katie has admitted she wants to go back to being Jordan and her behaviour since splitting from Pete has been wild, to say the least. She's gone back to her pneumatic glamour-model roots, getting drunk and posing erotically.

'From being a respected self-made entrepreneur, some people – young women and mothers, in particular – have turned against her. Some things being written and said are fairly vitriolic – and, of course, companies do not want to be associated with someone the public dislike. Crucially, they invested in Katie Price, not Jordan. While she will obviously continue with her own brand products, others are in serious jeopardy.'

What seemed to be upsetting Katie more than anything else was that Pete was getting all the sympathy, although he had actually been the one to leave. Indeed, she said as much on her Twitter site: 'Pete being a true c**t to me. He left me, not me leave him. I want a drink. I want to get off my nut. Let's go to the bar and get on with it.'

In its crudity, that message wasn't going to win her many fans, however. Nor did her subsequent behaviour, when she described in graphic detail how she and Anthony had not actually consummated the relationship, before continuing, 'If I say to Ant, "If I stay another night, will you sleep with me?" do you think he will? In fact, I think I *will* stay another night. Yes, that's what I am going to do!' she proclaimed, before chanting, 'We are staying another night, we are staying another night in Ibiza!'

But her cohorts, a little anxious now about what was going on, were none too thrilled.

'Don't be stupid, Katie,' said one. 'We are going home. You need to get ready for the kids.'

'OK, but I am still going to get drunk,' announced Katie, before she and her group spent the rest of the evening running up and down the corridors, banging on people's doors. It did not go down well with the other guests.

Finally, it was time to go home. The following day, the party arrived back at Gatwick, and the next day Katie set out for her usual riding lesson with her dressage instructor, Andrew Gould. Now back in the UK, it had been brought home to her quite how much damage the visit to Ibiza had caused her image: the children were still in Cyprus with Pete, and there had been a good deal of muttering in various quarters that they might be better off staying with him than returning to their errant mum.

Katie, as was her wont, was totally unrepentant. 'I am a good mum,' she said sharply. 'I've had a great time and people can slate me all they like. I work hard, I'm a mum; I'm a young woman and I'm going through a split. I bet you loads of women would do exactly the same thing.'

And that, as far as the Ibiza jaunt was concerned, was that. Except that it wasn't. Various elements continued to come to light, the first being that Anthony appeared to be seeing a new woman, Joanne Hunt, a dancer he met in the Eden nightclub in San Antonio.

'Yeah, we had a thing together,' said Joanne, who was based on the island. 'Anthony's a great guy. Of course I like him. I spoke to him yesterday and he told me nothing went on between him and Katie, and everything's been blown out of proportion.'

This seemed highly likely. Despite the best efforts in some quarters to portray the rivalry between the two women as some sort of catfight, Katie herself had admitted that she and Anthony had never actually consummated their relationship, which had clearly been little more than a holiday fling. She had wanted to show Pete that she was perfectly capable of having a good time without him (which she did, albeit, perhaps, a little too enthusiastically). Anthony, meanwhile, had clearly enjoyed all the attention. Rather like with a very different woman some years previously, Princess Diana, the men who hung around Katie got to bathe in her reflected glory – although, as with Diana, it tended not to last.

What was perhaps more surprising, and not reported until some time afterwards, was that Katie actually *did* have a fling with someone she met in Ibiza, although this wasn't to take off until she was back in the UK. In the wake of the break-up, her first real affair was with Andre Pinto, a 25-year-old Brazilian banker originally from Sao Paolo but resident in London for five years by the time they met.

By Pinto's own account, Katie pretty much used him on the rebound, in the early days of her hurt and shock over the split with Pete, and he ended up feeling more than a little upset. 'I was quite hurt and confused,' he revealed in the wake of the short fling. 'She used me for sex. She always said she didn't want a proper relationship. She treated me as a sex toy when it suited her, then dumped me.'

Katie first met Pinto in the Ibiza nightclub Amnesia, wearing the tiny gold one-piece that was extremely revealing and kept the photographers focused on her throughout the rest of the night. It was she who spotted Pinto, and she who made the first move. To her delight, he had no idea who she was.

'I didn't know her,' he admitted. 'She turned to her friends and said, "He doesn't have a clue – I love it." She said, "I'm Jordan. I'm a model and I'm here having fun." I thought she was really good-looking, with a nice smile and beautiful eyes. She was very small with big boobs. We started speaking and then we kissed. But her friends separated us, saying, "Don't do it here because of the paparazzi."'

Indeed, Katie spent the rest of her time in Ibiza partying without Pinto, but they did meet once they were both back in England, which is where the fling began. After a couple of dinners, the relationship was taken one step further at the home of Katie's friend Gary Cockerill.

'When we got there, we went straight to bed,' revealed Pinto. 'She took off her clothes and put knickers and a T-shirt on, and was waiting in bed for me. We started kissing and it went from there. She's a very good kisser – one of the best I've had.'

Katie did not, however, want to rush things. 'That night, she said we were not going to do anything because it was too early and she was not like that,' Pinto continued. 'She likes to show off, to play, to tease men, but she's not the kind of girl to sleep around with everybody. Then she said it was too hard to resist having me beside her. We started kissing and just got into it. It was really hot sex, but we only had it in the dark.'

Pinto paid two visits to Katie's home, the second being when Pete was looking after the children. Katie sent him a text: 'You are hornyx. Just ridden two horses gonna go training then shopping. Pete has kids tonightx. What are you up to later? Hey you wanna stay tonight? Could a friend drop you to mine?'

He could. 'We watched a movie together, then went to bed,' Pinto said. 'We didn't really watch the movie. We just played together and had fun. I liked her tattoos. I think she has a heart tattooed somewhere private, but I couldn't be sure because we always had sex in the dark. She liked to stare into my eyes while she did it.'

Katie was also quite open about the problems between herself and Pete. 'Katie told me he didn't really like going out,' continued Pinto. 'He wanted a wife to be inside the house, but she wanted to socialise. She said he always wanted to get her pregnant. She told me, "I love having a big family, but also wanted to have fun with my friends."'

But, to all intents and purposes, that was the end of it. The duo didn't see one another again, and shortly afterwards Pinto heard rumours that Katie had started to see cage fighter Alex Reid. 'It was then I knew it was over,' he said. 'I was disappointed I could not see her any more. I was having fun because she is fun and interesting. I never met Alex Reid. I don't want to meet him – I had a dream he beat me up and I'm scared of him.'

However, that was all still to come. Of course, the other man who was playing a big role in Katie's life was Pete, also back in the UK, and it didn't take long for matters to get even more bitter. The pair narrowly avoided bumping into one another at Nobu, the famous celebrity restaurant hangout in London. Then, one day, she brought Junior and Princess to Pete's new Sussex home at 3.15pm one day, only to discover that he wasn't there.

Pete was planning on taking the children out to celebrate Princess's birthday, and was more than a little bemused to find Katie on his case: arriving back about 20 minutes later, he said, 'It's supposed to be 4pm, so why did you have to come so early?' But he wasn't calm all the time, writing in his *New* magazine column that when he saw what Katie had been getting up to in Ibiza: 'I thought she was a disgrace.'

Meanwhile, she herself was backing away from it

all. There had been rumours linking her with ex-boyfriend Matt Peacock, but she insisted that she had had a fling with neither Anthony nor Matt. 'Jordan isn't back!' she said. 'I'm Katie Price.'

Indeed, she was, but, as the world was now beginning to realise, Katie did seem to have an increasingly split personality, veering wildly from one extreme of behaviour to the next. Katie and Jordan were both in there, making various appearances as circumstances demanded. And, as for Pete – well, the marriage wasn't merely over: all-out war had just begun.

CHAPTER THREE

The Heat Is On

If there had been any chance of reconciliation, although it was always unlikely, Katie's holiday in Ibiza put paid to that. Whatever the truth about what she did when she was away, the public perception was that, in the wake of the split, Katie was running completely wild. And the competition between the pair looked set to worsen. Even within the framework of their marriage, this had been an element, but now they were no longer a couple it seemed there was a real race on to see who remained most popular. And to Katie's utter astonishment, Pete seemed to be winning.

Given that when they got together Katie's star was

very much in the ascendant, while Pete's was on the wane, Katie clearly thought that the natural order, as she perceived it, was about to right itself. But it didn't. On the contrary, there had been a huge groundswell of public support for Pete, while Katie was seen to be the one behaving badly. One sign of this came in early July 2009, when he was signed up as the face of Christian Audigier, to model the Ed Hardy range. The deal, said to be worth €700,000, was a very prestigious one, too: in the past, Christian had used such huge names as Madonna and Michael Jackson to model his clothing range, so Pete was up there in very good company indeed.

But he was quite genuinely suffering, too. One of the great tragedies about the split was that it was making both Katie and Pete so miserable, but there was no going back. The division was too great, the bitterness too deep now, and so they battled on, both feeling dreadful and yet, in Pete's case at least, adamant that it really was the end.

Appearing on Chris Moyle's show on Radio 1, Pete revealed the full extent of his devastation, explaining that it would be impossible for him to form a new relationship with someone else just yet. 'I know my kids are probably listening,' he said. 'I wouldn't want to say anything negative about Mama. I'll be honest –

it's been the worst two or three months of my life. Then again, you've just got to get on with it, really. I've obviously never mentioned the reasons, but it's not just a reason. You don't just go with one reason, there's a number of things. I don't think that there is even one little bit in my head that can think of someone else, to be honest. My head's not even gone there yet, not even near it.'

Of course, this was in marked contrast to Katie's way of getting over the split, and it went down very well with the public. Peter Andre had always come across as a fundamentally decent man, but here was proof, as never before. The willingness to talk about his own pain, the desire to put his children first and to try to shield them from what was going on, combined with his reluctance to start a new relationship at this early stage, all marked him out as a thoroughly nice guy. And so public opinion began to shift in his direction in many ways: while Katie had always been the dominant force in the marriage, the strength of her personality towering over his own, Pete finally began to emerge from her shadow to stand before the public in his own right. Ever since they met, all those years previously in the jungle, he'd had to play second fiddle. That simply wasn't happening any more.

A further sign of public support came in July when Pete went to present an award at the O2 Silver Clef Awards in aid of the Nordoff-Robbins charity at London's Hilton Hotel. Denise Van Outen introduced him to an audience that included Gary Barlow, Lulu, Madness, the Stereophonics, Katherine Jenkins, Brian Wilson and Queen. 'Who's on Team Andre then?' she bellowed.

It turned out that everyone was. To Pete's utter bemusement, as he made his way towards the stage, all those present rose to give him a standing ovation, cheering, whooping and hollering as he passed by. Everyone was determined to shake his hand to show their support, while Pete looked absolutely staggered by it all. Eventually, he got to the stage, where he presented N-Dubz with Best Digital award.

It was exactly what Pete needed. 'People like Brian May and Gary Barlow are guys I really respect, so it's amazing to be a part of it,' he reflected afterwards. 'I can't believe how nice all these guys have been to me – I really wasn't expecting any of it. I'm slightly in shock.'

Others were taken aback, too. 'In the history of the Awards, we've never had a reaction quite like that,' said a fellow diner. 'Pete got mobbed and couldn't believe he received a standing ovation from some of the biggest and most respected names in the industry.'

And, of course, no one was more aware of what had happened that night than Katie. She was still very thrown by how it was all playing out. Meanwhile, there was a rumour that, to repair the damage to her image, she might start her own charity – one name mooted was The Katie Price Foundation – and she made a public appearance as the official patron of the Duke of Essex Polo Trophy, at a fundraiser in conjunction with VISION, a charity for blind, visually impaired and dyslexic children.

'She may have been acting more like an out-of-control glamour model of late, but, behind the glitz, she's a mother and has a heart,' said an insider. 'And she wants to help other parents like her, who are less fortunate.'

The event was held at Gaynes Park, Epping, and other celebrities there included Jack Tweed, Calum Best and Penny Lancaster.

It was Katie acting as Katie, rather than Jordan again, but Jordan still surfaced so regularly that she undid all the good work she'd done practically every time she opened her mouth. One minute Katie would be attending events such as this or looking after her children, or working hard, as she always had done, and getting on with her life; the next Jordan would be getting drunk, abusing or snogging strangers she'd met in bars. She might have been behaving so wildly because she was deeply upset, but, as Katie knew (and Jordan didn't), the mother of three small children simply can't be seen to be behaving like that.

All the while, a reminder was playing out on the TV screens about how it had all gone so badly wrong. The final instalment of *Katie and Peter: Stateside* screened in early July and made for uncomfortable viewing. 'I haven't enjoyed it here,' announced Katie on the screen. 'Everything went wrong.'

'The marriage didn't,' said Pete, although, alas, that most certainly wasn't the case any more.

And viewers were reminded quite how tense matters had become as the duo piled rubbish on a bonfire.

'Anything you want to burn?' Katie asked Pete.

'Yeah, you,' he replied.

In retrospect, of course, this was a turning point. The marriage staggered on for a short time afterwards, but it was that particularly vicious onscreen row in the shop, in which Pete and Katie argued with one another about which of them was the better known, that brought it all home that, finally, their relationship was truly over. Quite frequently, the constant bickering turned nasty; there was nothing gentle or tender about the way in which they were now relating to one another – indeed, even before the split they appeared to be at war. They also seemed to act as irritants towards one another: their mere presence together seemed to incite the other to unkindness and irritation. Looking back, that series quite clearly showed the writing was on the wall.

And now, of course, it was all out in the open, with some people joining Team Katie while others opting for Team Pete: the feuding was becoming vicious and it was very difficult for friends and acquaintances to continue to get along with them both. But one person who refused to be drawn into taking sides was Girls Aloud singer Sarah Harding, who had been a bridesmaid at the wedding. She was friends with them both, and was attempting to stay that way – which was perhaps why she didn't see Katie when the two of them were in Ibiza at the same time.

'It's so sad,' she said. 'I really hoped it wasn't permanent and wanted to get them back together. They have both been good friends to me in the past.

'I had a really hard time when I split up with Mikey Green and I'll never forget everything they did for me. Whenever I was feeling low, they'd invite me around to stay in their house to have a break from it all. Pete would put the kettle on and Katie would order in some Chinese, and we'd chat all night. They have both been good friends to me, so I'm not going to be drawn into the Team Katie or Team Pete thing. Whatever happened was between them.

'I've been in touch with them and said I'm here for both of them. But it doesn't look like they will get back together now, which is a shame. Some people said it was strange that I didn't go out with Katie in Ibiza, but it wasn't like that. We were in touch on the phone and met up in private. We talked about how she was feeling. I just wanted to make sure she was OK. It's not nice when something like this happens. I just hope that they are both OK.'

As Katie and Pete began to get used to life apart, there was, of course, intense speculation about their future relationships. Katie's flings in Ibiza looked increasingly to have been a bid for attention rather than anything more, while Pete had gone on the record – and continued to do so – in saying that he wasn't prepared to be involved with anyone else while he was still involved with Katie. Such was the feeling of goodwill towards Pete, however, that there was a palpable desire for him to meet someone else, and for a very short time it seemed, rather surprisingly, that that someone might turn out to be reality-TV star Chantelle Houghton.

Pete had been rather reclusive after the split, but, in early July, he ventured out to a party, where he met Chantelle. Afterwards, he was fulsome in his praise. 'It was the first time I'd met her and she was a really lovely girl, a real sweetheart,' he said. 'It's funny because she's exactly how I expected her to be after seeing her on TV and reading interviews she's done. We had such a great night and I think she's looking great. It was the first time I've been out since the split, so it was really nice to spend it with such lovely people.'

Had anything more come of it – indeed, should anything more come of it – this would have been highly ironic: in the past, Katie had shown signs of being jealous of Chantelle. During Chantelle's brief relationship with the singer Preston, to whom she was married, it had seemed as if they might actually threaten Katie and Pete's position as the No. 1 showbiz partnership. It hadn't turned out that way, of course, not least because their particular union was even shorter than Katie and Pete's, but the attention paid to them had been enough to ruffle Katie's feathers. To have her estranged husband praising Chantelle so openly must have stuck in the craw.

Even so, she was initially (rather unusually) gracious about it in public. 'I've been told by more than one person that Chantelle Houghton has been seen going into Pete's house on more than one occasion,' she said. 'It seems like her and Pete could be in a relationship. If they are, I'm happy for them. I think she's a good-looking girl – she seems nice and I hope they're happy, just as long as he's with someone who is nice to our kids. Good luck to them.'

It was a wise attitude to take, though not one that was subsequently necessary, given that the relationship never really took off. Besides, Katie was more than capable of holding the world's attention on her own. And it wasn't long before Katie was heard describing Chantelle as 'an ugly version of me'. This was more what she really felt: Katie had been perfectly open about the fact that she had suffered from jealousy just as much as Pete ever did when they were together. How she would have felt had anything serious come of the relationship was not that hard to guess.

Still, it was a nice diversion for her ex, and Pete was also feeling better about himself in other ways, too. 'Since the gym has been installed at my new home, I've not stopped working out,' he said. 'My brother Mike and I have been skipping, running and lifting weights. I've been pictured quite a lot lately, and, while people have been very complimentary, I'm nowhere near how I want to look. After losing that weight, I am now determined to build myself up again so I looked ripped. Maybe not quite like I was in the "Mysterious Girl" video, though!'

Despite the fact that she was being pretty gracious about the non-existent relationship with Chantelle, clearly Katie was still smarting about the fact that the public seemed to be so very much on Pete's side. Around this time, she began to talk about doing an interview with Piers Morgan so that everyone could judge for themselves who was in the right (or wrong).

'It's about time I put my side across about all the unfair things that have been said about me in the press,' she announced. 'I'm due some respect. I'm the one who was dumped.

'If it's on TV, people will be able to see I'm not a mess – far from it, I'm the happiest I've been in ages. They'll be able to see I'm not lying and I'm not acting. There will be some home truths – Pete is not as innocent as he's making out. People will be shocked when they know the truth.'

Initially, there was a cautious reaction to that particular idea. Enough dirt had already been thrown in public: was it really a good idea to go on television and throw some more? But there was a precedent, after all – none other than Princess Diana had gone on BBC's *Panorama* to open her heart about the harsh treatment she felt she had received. But Katie was in a very different position from Diana – not only was she not married to the heir to the throne, but there were not three people in what had been a fairly brief marriage – although, in a strange way, there were parallels between the two women.

Both had overcome some considerable adversity, although poor Diana's life was to be cut off when she was still so young, and both had an ability to make other women relate to them. Neither Diana nor Katie was in any way ordinary, the former by nature of her aristocratic heritage and stunning personal charisma, the latter through the sheer force of her determination, work ethic and achievements, but they made women in the street feel that they shared something in common. And for all the eyebrows being raised over Katie's wild behaviour, she had lost none of her ability to make other women feel that she was one of them. After all, many marriages break down and, as she was at pains to emphasise, it was Pete who had been the one to walk out, not Katie. And so, perhaps understandably, she wanted to get the message across.

Shortly afterwards, the interview most certainly

took place and Katie did indeed deliver her bombshell. It was indicative of a pattern that was to develop over the coming months: one sensational revelation followed another, keeping the estranged couple well and truly in the headlines (especially Katie's side of it), while playing out the drama for all the world to see.

In this, the first of Katie's really explosive revelations, it emerged for the first time that she had suffered a miscarriage shortly before the split. The pregnancy initially brought the two some degree of joy: there had been problems in the relationship, after all, and a new child was seen as heralding a new dawn. Perhaps the only thing that Katie and Pete really did have in common by this stage was their love of children and so both were at first delighted by the news, but it was not to be.

Their joy was short-lived, for Katie miscarried in the first, it was quickly becoming apparent, of a series of life-changing events in her life. Shortly afterwards, Katie and Pete famously ran the London Marathon together – and then came the break. There had been a huge amount of upheaval in a very short space of time.

'Even though we were still bickering, we were happy because it's a baby,' Katie explained to Piers in the interview which was broadcast on 11 July.

'Emotionally, for any woman to have a baby die, run the Marathon and then your husband wants a divorce and then split up, that's a lot for someone to take in.'

It was indeed, and it was also an explanation of how she went on to lose so much weight. Until then, the public had only known about the breakdown of the marriage: they had been unaware of what was happening behind the scenes.

Katie first suspected that she might be pregnant while they were still in the United States. 'I couldn't wait to get back home to get a scan,' Katie told Piers. 'I couldn't do it in America because, everywhere we went, we were getting followed by paparazzi and I didn't want them to see me go in to have a scan.

'[But] we had the scan and the doctor said he can't see a heartbeat. So he done some bloods and, three days later, he called me up and said, "It could still be alive." I knew I had to do the Marathon in a week's time, so my head was going because I thought, I've got to do the Marathon, I can't let people down.

'He said, "Come back on the Saturday, we'll do some more bloods." Over the weekend, the doctor phoned and said, "It's really good news. There's some kind of pregnancy there. Come back Monday." So I went in on Monday, and it was on the screen and he said, "No, it has died, it's gone." He said, "Well,

It didn't take long for the press to discover that Katie had a new man in her life. Cage fighter Alex Reid was soon to become a regular fixture.

Katie is an accomplished equestrian and is pictured above with her riding instructor Andrew Gould. Rumours of an affair between the two have always been denied by both parties.

Katie gets out and about to promote her various business ventures.

Above: The launch of her latest novel, *Sapphire*, was never going to be low-key affair.

Overleaf: Showing off the latest additions to her equestrian range of clothing.

Working hard to maintain her enviable figure while out running with her brother Danny.

Making an
entrance at
The Duke of
Essex Polo
Cup.

Above: Girls' night out – Katie gets a helping hand from security as she leaves the Dorchester Hotel in London.

Below: Girls' night in – having a heart-to-heart with the *Loose Women*.

The new romance blossoms as Katie and Alex spectate at a polo match in Spain.

we can terminate it tonight." So I had to be there – I had to be put to sleep and have it terminated.'

Whatever anyone thought of her subsequent behaviour, this was clearly a terrible blow and she still had the commitment to run the Marathon before her.

'I'd half thought it would be all right and I thought, I've lost another baby,' Katie continued. "I thought, I can't let anyone down. I just wanted to say to people, "Just leave me alone, I've just lost a baby, I'm bleeding," but I can't say it because, you know, it's private.'

Katie and Pete did go ahead and run the Marathon, but she didn't find it easy. She'd only just had the miscarriage, which no one knew about, and there were real concerns about her health. 'When you've had an anaesthetic, it knocks you anyway, let alone emotionally,' she continued.

'I'm thinking, Oh my God! because we wanted the baby, and it had died and there was nothing I could do. It's dangerous to run when you're bleeding that much – you can get a blood clot. On the day of the Marathon, I keep going to the toilet because I keep checking to see if I'm bleeding. I'm trying to keep myself together, not to cry.'

It was just two weeks afterwards that Pete said he wanted to leave.

'I was so into him, so in love with him,' said Katie sadly. 'I can honestly say it was love at first sight. We had great sex, we done everything together – we just had a complete laugh. I never, ever in a million years thought I'd divorce. I didn't get married to divorce. Never! He was my total everything and I loved him till the day that obviously he split up with me. Even when the statement was put out about us, I started thinking, Shit, this is really it!'

Too much togetherness had been part of the problem, she felt.

'When you're working with someone all the time, when you come home, what do you talk about?' she asked. 'It was if like 24/7 we were stuck together – that's not healthy.'

As for the other stories, especially the rumours of her relationship with Andrew Gould, Katie tackled this head-on.

'Pete had it in his head that I fancied him, he fancied me,' she said. 'Every time I'd go to the horse, I'd come back in a good mood and Pete would look at it as if Andrew's making me in a good mood. So it grew in his head until he ended up thinking something was going on. I told him, "There is nothing going on." But by then, of course, it was too late.'

Then there was the recent holiday in Ibiza.

THE HEAT IS ON

'When I have a drink, I want to take my clothes off,' admitted Katie, in a rather resigned tone. 'I don't smoke, I don't take drugs, but occasionally I'm a binge drinker: I'm an exhibitionist, I am a nightmare. As for Ibiza, I was always going there to do my calendar shoot. I went out about three nights, the other nights I went for dinner. What do you go to Ibiza for? To eat scones and drink tea?'

It was a good point, but she had perhaps forgotten that everything she was doing was in the full glare of the camera and, eventually, her antics would be seen by the same public who had regarded her as the doting wife and mother not so long before.

And, if she wanted even more attention to be brought on herself, that interview most definitely did the trick. The shock news about the miscarriage made the front pages and there was certainly a great deal more sympathy than had been shown publicly before. It was also to emerge that this was not Katie's first miscarriage: for some time now, the couple had been trying for another child and she had miscarried previously. Whatever her wild behaviour might say about her, here was a woman in pain.

Naturally, not everyone was on her side. Pete's camp was livid about it all, not least because he considered that the miscarriage had been a private trauma for them both and he didn't want the world knowing their news. If Katie had been trying to win the public sympathy vote by talking about the miscarriage, it hadn't actually worked that well, given that most people were still on Pete's side. Even so, he was not pleased.

'The fact she has gone public has stunned him to the core,' said a friend. 'This is a private matter that should never have come to light. Katie said she was going to keep a dignified silence, yet goes on TV telling seven million people about their personal life. He's disgusted by her behaviour. As far as he's concerned, this is the lowest of the low.'

And it wasn't long before Pete himself was speaking out.

'I was shocked and stunned by how far she went,' he said. 'This information should have remained private.' He enforced the point when a fan gave him her good wishes. 'Please do not believe the bullshit my wife will be telling you on TV tonight,' he said, before heading off to lunch with his parents, who were in town to support him.

'Pete's parents flying over is just the tonic he needed,' admitted a friend. 'He is devastated over Katie's decision to go public with the details of her miscarriage. As far as he's concerned, this shows how low she's prepared to stoop. Pete knows Kate is a master media manipulator and will do anything to protect her image. He's sad to see she's brought the death of their unborn child out into the public arena.'

This, of course, only made matters worse. Whatever one of them said, the other disputed, with both now seemingly incapable of seeing any kind of reason. The battle was both personal and public: not only did each of them want the upper hand, but they were eager to emerge as the more popular one, too. Pete was angry that Katie had spoken out; now Katie was angry that Pete was angry.

'Just remember who dumped who,' she told a friend, and added, 'Peter seems to forget he demanded a divorce 12 days after I had a miscarriage. Those are the facts, and for him to cast himself as innocent and upset in all of this is unbelievable. He is not the good guy everyone is making out – in fact, the opposite is true.'

Now the two camps were truly at war, as well as the principal players, and a friend of Katie's backed her up. 'Throughout their marriage, they've lived in the public eye, 24/7, and have shared intimate details of their lives to millions of people,' he said. 'For Peter to turn around now and say her behaviour was out of order is totally unreasonable. It's almost as if he's trying to divert attention away from the fact he dumped her so soon after she lost a baby. In the cold light of day, that is inexcusable – at least in Katie's eyes. For Katie to be painted as the villain of the piece by Peter's camp is hypocritical to the extreme.'

They were at each other's throats, with neither prepared to back down.

Given the circumstances, when they next met – a couple of days later – the atmosphere was cool, to put it mildly. Katie took the children to stay with their father at his rented house in Hove, but this was not exactly making an effort to calm matters down.

'Here, she has a full nappy,' she snarled, as she handed over Princess Tiaamii. 'Clear up your own shit!' With that, she was off, reality-TV crew in tow.

Pete kept his cool and didn't lash out in return, taking the children out for a day in Hastings, followed by a barbecue with his mother and brother. But an observer revealed what was really going on.

'Pete couldn't even look at Katie, he was just pleased to see the children,' he said. 'She made the comment about the nappy and then asked if he had enough clothes for the kids. Pete said he had plenty, and scooped up the children and gave them a big kiss and made a fuss over them, so they didn't think anything was wrong. He tried to ignore all the cameras, but he was obviously annoyed that she had turned up with them. They didn't even discuss the TV interview – it was awkward and frosty.'

Various allegations of hypocrisy had been flying from Katie's camp on the subject of Pete's objection to her speaking out publicly when their whole married life had been one giant reality-TV show. Indeed, it seemed Pete was beginning to question quite how wise it had been to live like that. He, too, gave an interview, in his case to *This Morning* on ITV, with presenters Phillip Schofield and Fern Britton. This was a show on which he had appeared many times in the past with his estranged wife, and it was clearly a difficult time for him. Not only was he questioning the wisdom of the way the two had lived together, but he was also, despite everything, still trying not to get into too public a slanging match.

'I do look back at the times we all had here and it was fantastic,' he admitted. 'There are fantastic memories here. [But] showing your life so publicly is a mistake sometimes, but I blame myself as much as anyone else. I did mention yesterday that I'm between a bit of a rock and a hard place because, when you don't speak, you only hear one side of the story. But, when you do speak, you have to think long term.

'Right now, it would benefit me to speak and there's a lot I would want to say, but, long term, I know the kids are going to grow up and look back at everything. Yes, I have lost a lot of weight, but after today, judging by all the cakes that are being made, I think that might change.'

But it was too late to worry about all that now. Ostensibly, he was on the show to promote his new single, 'Behind Closed Doors', though, clearly, he was still brooding about the past. 'What's done is done, you have to move on,' he said. 'I don't say that happily, I just say it because it is what it is.'

There was a tinge of regret in his tone, however, and a real sadness about the past.

CHAPTER FOUR

Camp Katie

Always one to look to the future, Katie took a short break in Los Angeles. It was her first visit back to the city since the split was announced and she held a series of meetings with television agents about future work. This was a fruitful time, leading to some speculation about possible film work, and it also gave her a chance to relax: she was pictured having lunch with David Walliams, who had recently filmed a sketch mocking Katie and Pete for his new show. Clearly, there were no hard feelings there. Indeed, behind the scenes, she and Walliams were fast becoming close friends.

The trip to LA passed off without incident. It had

been rumoured that she originally wanted to return to Ibiza, but her managers had persuaded her to think again, fearing a repeat of the earlier debacle. As it was, there now seemed to be a chance that she might appear in a UK version of *Baywatch*, to be produced by David Hasselhoff himself.

'I've been thinking about basing a new show over here [Britain]. It would be called *UK-Watch*, and Jordan is certainly feisty and has curves in all the right places,' the Hoff revealed.

In many ways, this would be the perfect role for Katie. The original *Baywatch* had, of course, made Pamela Anderson a globally famous celebrity and the similarities between herself and Katie were obvious of course – surgically enhanced, and very noticeable, breasts. Katie was not quite in the same league, yet: undoubtedly, she was a major star with a huge following, but she hadn't quite gained the global appeal of Pamela, and she had yet to become internationally known. It was another good reason to be in LA, too: if she could crack America, she had a chance of becoming part of the international A-list, along the lines of her erstwhile nemesis Victoria Beckham, but she wasn't quite there.

Pete, meanwhile, was still in the UK, looking after the children and doing all he could to keep everything calm. He took the children to have their faces painted and joined in, good-naturedly allowing himself to be painted as Spider Man. The kids were in raptures, but their parents were still barely able to communicate. And so the war between the two went on.

But Katie wasn't the only one to be focusing on her career: Pete was doing exactly the same, too. He had a new album, *Revelation*, and a new single, and he – as well as the public – was focusing on that. Of course, a great deal of attention was paid to the single, 'Behind Closed Doors'. It was the latest step in his musical comeback, but a lot rested on the track: was the song about the break-up? Now that he was no longer half of the country's most popular couple, would he be able to make it on his own?

Pete himself had said that he wrote the songs when he was happy and that it would be odd to hear them all again. 'The album has been pretty much finished for four months,' he said, on the eve of its release. 'It will be weird listening to some of the songs on the radio because I wrote them before we broke up. I wanted to put out an album about my own emotions – it was like therapy. Instead of writing a diary, I wrote songs.'

He certainly wouldn't be the first to use personal

heartbreak as the inspiration for his music and, in many ways, it had proved a cathartic process for him. Whatever the rights and wrongs about what had happened between him and Katie, Pete had seen an initial resurgence in his popularity that must have been fuelled by interest in the relationship, but now he was proving that he really could make it on his own. And, similarly to Katie, he was finding refuge in his work. It had been an enormously difficult period, but at least he still had his music and it was serving as a channel for some of his emotions, however negative they might be.

Pete continued to be reflective, however, clearly now believing that it had been a mistake to allow the cameras quite so much access into the couple's lives as they had.

'I can't think about another relationship,' he said. 'I won't be going near anyone for a long time. For the past five years, it's been very public and I used to be a private person. I enjoy the industry now and I can't complain, but it doesn't have to be so public.' Of course, it didn't – but it had been. And there was no going back on the recent past.

Katie, it would appear, did not feel the same. On her return to the UK, there was another burst of wild behaviour, similar to the antics in Ibiza, except that she was now back on her own soil. It was also to be the occasion when she would link up with Alex Reid, although that was not to become obvious just yet. However, it was also a reminder of just how wild and out of control she could become once she allowed the Jordan persona to take over, and it was not the kind of act that the public relished her putting on.

On 19 July, it was her great friend Michelle Heaton's 30th birthday and Katie pulled out all the stops: for a start, there was the matter of her outfit, a very revealing black basque and tutu. The ensemble left so little to the imagination that she was in danger of upstaging the birthday girl: subtlety was clearly not to be the order of the day on this particular night out. Then, in a development horribly reminiscent of Ibiza, there was her unpleasant behaviour with fans when the proceedings kicked off at 10.45pm at the Mayfair Hotel.

Indeed, for someone who understood so well the importance of the public image, Katie could be remarkably unpleasant when it came to dealing with members of the public who dared to approach her on her nights out. Another woman was also there at the hotel, celebrating her 30th, and approached the revellers.

'The girl came over to Jordan and Michelle's table, and said she just wanted to say "Happy birthday" to Michelle, as it was her birthday too,' said an onlooker. 'But Jordan just snapped at her.'

It was an astonishing way to behave, especially given the fact that this kind of outburst had landed her in trouble not so long ago. While she hadn't gone that far on this particular occasion, she was still being unnecessarily unpleasant to someone who was, after all, doing her no harm. This might well have been because Katie started off with a male fan base, when she inhabited the persona of Jordan, and had not quite got used to the idea that women were the ones who looked up to her now, but they had to be treated a little differently. They empathised with Katie for all sorts of reasons, but she had to be seen to be doing so in return.

Not that night, however, and festivities continued apace. The assembled company went on to Studio Valbonne, where the order of the day was vodka cocktails and mini smoked salmon bagels in the VIP lounge. On the stroke of midnight, they moved into the main section of the bar, where Michelle was presented with a magnum of champagne and a huge birthday cake. Another three clubs followed in short succession: Mo*vida, The Shadow Lounge and

Balans. It was a raucous occasion, much enjoyed by everyone concerned.

And, even though she had to get her act together and learn when to calm it down, Katie certainly enjoyed the fact that she continued to shock. She managed to cause a rumpus by proclaiming to *Glamour* magazine, 'I wouldn't mind a bit of Simon Cowell.' It was not known whether the sentiment was returned. Nor was Cowell the only man that she had her eyes on: 'There's actually quite a few footies that I'd do,' she said. 'I'd probably go back to Frank Lampard, finish what I started.' Lampard's opinion wasn't canvassed, but the message was clear: Katie was out there and raring to go. She was a single woman once more, with as much of an eye for an attractive man as she'd ever had, and she was over Pete.

Actually, she almost certainly wasn't over him, but that's not what she wanted the world to believe. She was keen to prove that she was her own woman, ready to get out there again.

Meanwhile, the war between them continued apace. As was happening so frequently in those days, Pete was also out around the time that Katie was very publicly partying, but taking part in a totally different activity. He was on stage at Western-super-Mare on T4 on the Beach, which was where he would premiere his new single, although it was not the most auspicious of occasions. The weather was awful and Pete was getting drenched, almost falling off the stage at one point.

'I was a little nervous before I went on stage,' he admitted, but he got through it all, supported, as ever, by the massive goodwill of the crowd.

Indeed, his natural charm and affability was such that he turned what was a near catastrophe into little more than a talking point. Pete was in the middle of 'Behind Closed Doors' when he missed his footing and fell off the stage, into the middle of a crowd, which promptly mobbed him. He carried on singing and managed to climb back on stage, at which point his earpiece came out and he was unable to stay in tune with the music. It said something about his popularity that the audience just went along with it all.

'One minute he was bouncing around the stage having the time of his life,' said Carly Wells, a member of the audience. 'The next he was flat on his face in front of us. There was a loud gasp as he fell – the stage was quite high up and it looked quite nasty. But he just picked himself up, brushed his trousers down and got on with it. I was quite close and could see he was smiling – so I don't think he was badly hurt. Just his pride, maybe.'

But even his pride wasn't that badly dented – Pete could feel the goodwill emanating from the audience, proof that they really were on his side.

Meanwhile, back in Camp Katie, she was giving another television interview, this time to ITV's *Loose Women*, but was striking a more measured tone. Indeed, she was talking increasingly frequently about the marriage, very much on a charm offensive in order to get the public on her side. Clearly, she still didn't understand why she, the person who had been left, was on the receiving end of criticism and was continuing in her attempt to win people round.

'I was always expecting it to end,' she said, revealing that the marriage had been in trouble for at least two years, and that now, of course, the couple had to decide what to do about the children. 'Junior sort of knows there's something going on. My mum and dad split up when I was young, but, from Pete's side, and my side, there's so much love going on. I think kids need that support.'

She was also adamant that the two of them had worked hard at the marriage, never intending things to turn out as they had. 'For two years, me and Pete – we tried, like any marriage,' she said. 'You do try. It was like, "If you push your luck, I will finish with you." So I suppose I got to a stage where I was always expecting it. I did all my crying while I was married, but I never wanted a failed marriage.'

Sadly, this was what she'd got. Soon, however, very soon, Katie would start to look for romance elsewhere.

When the couple first split, there was some doubt as to whether, apart, they would be able to maintain the high profile they had shared together. But the doubters were proved utterly wrong. Such was the interest in what Katie and Pete were doing that they were now, if anything, attracting even more attention than ever before, and that focus came from some very unexpected quarters.

Take the actor Rupert Everett. He would have been one of the last people assumed to be associated with Katie under normal circumstances, yet he appeared to be as fascinated by her as anyone else.

'Jordan is one of those people who has integrity,' he said in an interview with the *Mirror* in which the subject of fame was being discussed. 'She is not dishonest about what she is doing. She should make hay while the sun shines. Her eldest son is severely disabled – she needs the money for the future. She is very beautiful and even the books that she may or may not have written have been a success. She has achieved more than a lot of other people.

'If I had the choice of being on a desert island with Jordan or Gwyneth Paltrow, I would choose Jordan ... She's treated like a quasi-hooker, whereas Gwyneth is seen as the patron saint of good living ... I would much rather have Jordan any day!'

Clearly, Rupert was a member of Club Katie, who incidentally was delighted when she heard about her new admirer. But, closer to home, friends of the duo were also having to make difficult choices; as with many break-ups, it was proving very tricky to stay friends with both. One of the people to discover the truth of this was Katie's great friend Gary Cockerill, a make-up artist: although he had become friendly with Pete and the duo attended his civil partnership ceremony with Phil Turner a few years previously, when he and Phil decided to renew their vows in August 2009, Pete did not make the guest list.

'Katie and Pete's mutual friends can see them separately, but, as they can't be in the same room together, their friends have the terrible decision to make,' said another friend. 'Gary is really close to both Katie and Pete. He has styled them both for years and has even lived with them in the past when he was in high demand. It was a tough decision to make, but they decided as a couple that their loyalties lay with Katie, and they didn't want their big day to be overshadowed by a showdown between the two.'

Nor was Katie simply a bystander for the proceedings: she played a role akin to that of bridesmaid. So it's easy to see why it might have been problematic had Pete been there.

And anyway, she herself was getting on with life, just as she always did. Breezily telling friends that she was planning on getting more Botox and a new tattoo, there were also hopes that she would land a role in the second *Sex and the City* movie. 'I recently went to LA, where I was doing my acting lessons for *Sex and the City 2*,' she said. 'They want a big-breasted English glamour girl and I have had the audition.'

Indeed, ever the pragmatic businesswoman, Katie was planning ahead. No one was more practical and realistic, and she would have been well aware that her time as a model was limited. Now in her thirties, she couldn't go on as she had been doing forever, which meant that other outlets must be found. Already, she did a huge amount of promotional work, had clothing lines that were now sold internationally and a whole library of books under her belt, but acting was something that would provide a whole new angle to her career. It was also a way of extending her international exposure and, if Katie got a role in the *Sex and the City* movie, she was guaranteed even more publicity than she usually generated. Life, in that sphere at least, looked good.

However, events were to take a far nastier turn for the worse. Until then, the split had mainly been a war of words between the couple, but towards the end of July 2009, Pete decided to get lawyers involved in a matter outside of simply finalising the details of the divorce. Without openly saying so, Katie had appeared on *GMTV* and implied that he might have been unfaithful. Pete, an avowed family man, who valued fidelity and who had publicly refused to take a new partner until the two were formally divorced, was outraged. He threatened legal action, and went publicly on the record. 'I've been 100 per cent faithful,' he said. 'Any reports suggesting otherwise are false.'

But this was an issue that would come up time and again in the following months. There was, in fact, no question about Pete's fidelity: no one ever seriously suggested that he might have been unfaithful to Katie; he had never been seen in compromising circumstances and so committed was he to the ideal of a good relationship that even now, when he was to all intents and purposes a free man, he still refused to get involved with anyone else until the divorce was finalised. But this was not the last time that Katie would hint darkly that all was not as it should have been. Perhaps it was all a bid to gain public sympathy, perhaps Katie had genuinely talked herself into believing that he might be seeing someone else, but all it did was to make it even more obvious that Pete had been a faithful spouse. He would hardly have threatened court action had there been any hint at all of wrongdoing. Yet again, through lashing out in her pain, Katie had only made the situation worse.

Certainly, the two seemed set on hurting one another as much as possible. Katie might have been getting riled because reports were circulating that Pete wanted to take the children to his homeland, Australia, although he was adamant that it would only be for a holiday, not a permanent relocation.

'I have this unbelievable desire to get the kids in a camper van and take them across Australia,' he admitted. 'It's my ultimate dream.' It was also, poignantly, where he and Katie first met in the Australian bush in *I'm A Celebrity*, and there was the feeling that he also wanted to show the children where their parents had first fallen in love.

However, the reports also set alarm bells ringing.

Even though Pete had made it clear that this was to be for only a short time, the unspoken implication was clear: if Katie behaved like a bad mother, he could go for custody, in which case he really might have been able to relocate. Nothing was said so openly, but the stakes appeared increasingly high. This was not just a question of Katie's standing in the public eye: it was also about her future with her children. She spoke of her pain at being branded a bad mother and her ex-husband first threatening to sue her, then talking about taking her children to the other side of the world, which would only grieve her more.

Nor were matters helped when someone else came forward to claim an Ibiza fling (of sorts) with Katie – except this time, it was a woman. Former *Playboy* Playmate Georgia Abalaru, who owned a villa on the island that was the backdrop to part of the photo shoot for Katie's calendar, and who was present for a good deal of the drunken carousing, refused to hold back on the details, too.

'She was really lovely and said she wanted to meet up with me again on a night out,' revealed Georgia. 'I couldn't refuse as I was a massive fan of hers from her TV show. She was a bit flirty, but I thought nothing of it because she knew I had a boyfriend.'

But a couple of days later, when the two met at the club Amnesia, it turned out to be more than that.

'Katie was in the VIP area with all her friends and it was getting close to 5am,' Georgia continued. 'I was wearing black latex leggings and a little black top, which she said was really pretty. She then lunged towards me and started snogging me as if it was the most natural thing in the world. She just lurched for me and stuck her tongue down my throat. I told her I had a boyfriend, but she just kept saying, "Fuck that!" Although she was all over quite a lot of the men there, it's fair to say she took a particular shine to me.'

So far, so silly: Katie, by now very drunk, could well have just been larking about. However, the scene suddenly turned darker and more bizarre. 'She started screaming that she liked being strangled,' said Georgia.

Hardly surprising, nor did things get any better. 'She started going on about how Peter couldn't handle her and asked me if I could handle her,' Georgia went on, after which Katie pointed to one of the men present. 'I just want to have a bit of sex because I haven't had sex for ages,' she said, but, when she learned that the man in question already had a girlfriend, she was equally forthright. 'Fuck your girlfriend, it's all about me!' she cried.

She was, of course, extremely drunk and went on to kiss three other men, who happened to be present.

'Katie was just pointing at men and they were being brought up to her,' recalled Georgia. 'It was like she was a queen choosing her subjects. She was all over them like a rash and loving all the attention.'

For once, the cameras weren't rolling, and Katie's management team clearly wanted to get her out of the way before any more damage could be done. When Katie finally decided that she wanted to return to her hotel, a stealth operation had to be quickly mounted.

'Katie had make-up smeared over her face,' said Georgia. 'She looked like a clown. They were terrified that she'd be photographed outside the club, but they got away with it. Her behaviour couldn't have been any more opposite after she had a drink. She was a different person to the one I met at the villa. She's a little mad, but she must have been hurting after breaking up with Peter. Perhaps me and her was just her way of letting off steam.'

Almost certainly, it was nothing more than that. Katie had plenty of other things to deal with, not least the fact that she was now taking acting lessons in a bid to further her career. Indeed, she had signed up with the Creative Artists Agency in Los Angeles, which also represented such stars as Brad Pitt, Will

Smith, George Clooney, Julia Roberts and Tom Cruise. 'She's aiming much higher than walk-on bimbo parts and we reckon she's a rough diamond, who can be shaped and polished for much better things,' said an agency insider.

But there was more on Katie's mind than just that.

By the end of July, speculation was rife that Katie had embarked on her first serious relationship since the split with Pete. The man in question was Alex Reid, a cage fighter and former actor, who had appeared on Channel 4's soap *Hollyoaks* as footballer Jason Cunliffe. He was now better known for his sporting abilities, working as 'The Detonator', but his return to acting would shortly spark a great deal of controversy. Nor were the public at all sure what to make of him (and, as time went on, details of his life became ever more outlandish and bizarre), but, if truth be told, he'd have had to make a huge effort to win public support, whatever he was like, because of one thing alone: he wasn't Pete.

There were mixed reports about when they'd met and, indeed, conflicting views about Alex's role in Katie's life, as he initially joined her entourage in a security role. But their involvement very quickly became much more than that. The two were spotted together at the Malmaison hotel in Liverpool, where

Katie was staying after a book signing for her latest novel *Sapphire*. 'They were sat with friends, but Jordan couldn't keep her hands off Reid,' said one observer. 'She was rubbing his leg up and down suggestively and kept whispering in his ear. She was literally draped over him. It was very dark in the bar, so they probably thought nobody would notice, but Jordan's teeth were gleaming and you could spot them a mile off. It was clear they needed to get a room. And when they got inside, there was a lot of noise, a constant banging.'

Another onlooker confirmed this. 'She seemed to get more and more slaughtered as the night went on,' he recalled. 'They started drinking at the Malmaison hotel, where they're staying. Then they went clubbing at Panacea till 2.30am and then on to the Circle Club till 4.30am. All the time, Alex was right by her side – even when they went for a kebab together at around 5am. By the time they got a cab home together, Katie was hammered. She looked to be lying with her legs across Alex, with him holding her up.'

It was because she'd been drinking, perhaps, that people didn't initially realise this was far more than just another session of falling about the place with a group of strange men. So many stories had emerged about Katie's behaviour in Ibiza that this, too, might have seemed simply another bout of wildness, but, in reality, she had found someone that she wanted to be with. It might have been a rebound relationship, but it was much more than just a fling.

Alex initially denied the rumours. He knew Katie, yes, but that was all there was to it.

'The truth is we *are* close,' he said. '[But] all that's been written about Katie and me is complete craziness. Our relationship is completely professional. Katie is trained by a friend of mine, and, through him, she asked me if I wanted to be her bodyguard. You could say that she decided to kill two birds with one stone.'

Asked if Katie wanted to learn cage fighting, he continued, 'Who knows? I would not rule it out. I think she would be interested in it for self-defence and fitness reasons.'

At first, no one seemed to know quite what to make of the new relationship, though one thing was certain – Alex Reid was a very different sort of man from Peter Andre. Quite how different remained to be seen, but in those early sightings, a cage fighter was pretty much the extreme opposite of a pop star. Exactly how the two fitted together was unclear. Indeed, some observers felt that this new relationship was a big mistake.

'Things just seem to go from bad to worse for Katie,' said one. 'More and more pictures of her out boozing till the early hours, dressed in skimpy outfits, drunk and in the company of different men will tip the balance in Andre's favour.'

And she was upsetting fans for different reasons, too. Never a modest dresser, Katie's outfits had recently plunged to new lows – literally, as far as the neckline on some of them was concerned. She was touring the country to promote her new book and, frequently, the audience that turned out to see her was full of very young girls while her own attire seemed more suited to the nightclub. One very daring black outfit, which showed off huge amounts of cleavage and boasted only the shortest of skirts, raised eyebrows, as did the blue sequinned leotard that she appeared in twice: with and without a blue tutu.

Natalie Jones, a mother-of-two who attended the book signings, was not impressed. 'Katie had become an inspiration to me – she seems to have been through a lot in her life,' she said. 'Since she left the Jordan image behind her, she had become well respected. But this outfit was just totally inappropriate: it looks like she was out for a night on the town in Ibiza. If I had known she was appearing as Jordan, I would never have brought my children along to this. You could see absolutely everything! It's obvious since she split from her husband she is just desperate for attention. She should stick with the image she had before, she would get a lot more respect that way.'

On the other hand, of course, Katie's interesting dress sense did ensure that she appeared almost constantly in the tabloids. Indeed, there was no aspect of her life that wasn't of almost total and overwhelming interest now: her clothes, her holidays, her choice of partners, all were obsessing the public. And that was another of the strange elements that now made up her life: while public sympathy might have been almost entirely with Pete, public fascination with Katie was just as strong as it had ever been. Ever since those very early days on the glamour circuit, her life had been extraordinary... It was that little bit more extraordinary now.

CHAPTER FIVE

Katie and Alex

And so it was that, a mere matter of months after the break-up of her relationship with Pete, Katie found someone new. She had needed something, or someone, to cheer her up and Alex was perfect: good-looking, manly and clearly as pleased to be with Katie as she was with him. Of course, he had a much more interesting past than anyone was aware of just yet, and he would go on to provide quite a few headlines in his own right, but that just added to the fascination for many. Certainly, Katie had found herself an interesting new man.

She was clearly increasingly wrapped up in her latest relationship. When Alex's 34th birthday came round, Katie gave him a £4,000 Chanel watch with a note that read: 'I feel a great connection with you'. As the couple continued to be photographed together, there was also some speculation that their acquaintance was not as new as it seemed, with some onlookers believing the duo had actually been in contact with one another for some time, although, of course, the romantic aspect to their relationship was a fresh spin.

'Katie's been in touch with Alex for a while,' said a friend. 'She got his number from Sol [Gilbert, her martial-arts trainer] when she saw a picture of him a year ago ... He's even been over when the kids have been home. Kate thinks Alex is the opposite to her ex – he's a fearsome opponent, a real animal, and would have Pete for breakfast. Alex is familiar with the showbiz circuit. In many ways, he's a lot like her.'

That was as maybe, but many people who were close – or had been – to the couple were stunned. Pete, utterly shocked by the turn of events, was said to be 'numb'. Even though he obviously couldn't have expected his ex to have forsaken all men after him, this was moving extremely fast. Nor was Marie Thornett particularly thrilled: she had been Alex's girlfriend for the past decade, and was as taken aback as anyone else. Indeed, she would cause severe embarrassment to the couple in the coming weeks, although for now she contented herself with simply talking about her shock.

'Alex never told me about him and Jordan,' she said in an interview with *Closer* magazine. 'I was so embarrassed as everyone else knew about it. I've hardly stopped crying since.' And Alex was not returning her calls, she continued, until finally, he 'pretended he didn't know what I was talking about. Eventually he said he didn't mean to hurt me. He was desperate to be famous – he's been working towards that for the last 10 years. Being with Jordan is a great opportunity for him to get known and I suppose he couldn't turn it down.'

It was a pretty bitter remark, but then, like everyone else in this sorry saga, Marie had been hurt. But she was right about one thing: Alex had been around for a long time now, and had tried on many occasions to get his lucky break. Indeed, it was beginning to emerge that he was no stranger to the world of showbusiness. Apart from his appearances in *Hollyoaks*, he had been Tom Hanks's body double in *Saving Private Ryan* and had taken minor roles in *Sliding Doors*, *Judge Dredd*, *Tomorrow Never Dies* and Stanley Kubrick's *Eyes Wide Shut*. All of this had led to a somewhat limited profile, but now, suddenly, everyone knew who Alex was.

Katie herself now felt the time was right to go public about her new man, although she was a little coy as to how far the relationship had progressed, initially talking about it mainly as a friendship.

'He is a fighter,' she revealed. 'He's a bit like me in that respect. Alex has been a huge support to me recently. I have known him a long time, but he's a good friend now. I'm having lots of fun at the moment, which I think I deserve after everything I've been through lately.'

She did indeed. However, this was not the first time that she had been linked to another man since the split, and so Katie clearly decided it was time to go on record about exactly what she had been getting up to recently, especially in Ibiza. And that meant Anthony Lowther. 'He's my friend too, but that's as far as it goes,' she continued. 'I had my picture taken with him a few times, that doesn't make him my boyfriend. I am enjoying being a single girl. I am focusing on my children, which I love. I've got lots of male friends, but I am well and truly single.

'Yes, I know lots of men and I get on very well with a lot of them, but I do not have a boyfriend. I just want to date a normal man now. I don't want anyone famous, I just want someone ordinary, like a builder or something. I want someone to love me for being me, someone not complicated – that's when I'm ready to get into another relationship.'

But things had clearly gone further with Alex than just friendship. The pair had been seen going into the same hotel bedroom, although a spokesman for Katie had an explanation. 'He makes Katie feel secure. He is a trained cage fighter and acts as extra security for her,' he insisted. 'She said she wants him there to keep her safe and he did accompany her into her room in Liverpool.'

Very soon, however, Katie and Alex would not be able to resist telling the world how happy they were together. Quite apart from the fact that the physical evidence was now making it clear that they were a couple – when they weren't seen going into the same hotel room, they were pictured all over each other – hardly 'just friends' behaviour. What's more, they were quickly in the throes of the first stages of a love affair, when it is almost irresistible not to talk about the beloved practically the whole time. Put simply, they wanted to boast about each other, because that is the nature of the early stages of a relationship. Besides, they had nothing to hide.

Other people were happy, too. Sol Gilbert, who had introduced them, was pleased about the development of the relationship. 'Alex is a very caring person and a great guy,' he said. 'He is one of my closest friends and Katie needs someone to look after her, so nothing would make me happier than if they stayed together.'

There was, of course, another element to all this – Pete. Was she really over him after such a short time apart? That was very unclear. Katie seemed to veer wildly between putting a very brave face on it and trying to win him back behind the scenes, but, for now, at least, she was adamant that her only concern was in what lay ahead.

'Splitting with Pete is the best thing that has ever happened to me,' she told one interviewer. 'There was a time when I was in pieces, but that's all behind me now. All the time I was with Pete, I was more concerned with making sure our marriage worked, but now I am focusing on me, my children and my career. I don't have to worry about making sure another person in my life is happy with what I am doing any more.'

Brave words, although not everyone was entirely convinced that that was how she really felt.

According to Katie, it was now her career that was the main concern, alongside her children. 'I'm trying to achieve a few more things in life that I'd put on the backburner while I was with Pete,' she continued. 'I had a great time when I was in LA, two weeks ago. There's something about America, I'm not sure what it is, but I love it. No, I'm not trying to be like Victoria Beckham, but, before you ask, I don't have a bad word to say against her any more, so don't even try and go there, girl!'

And that was another break with the past: Katie and Victoria supposedly had famously enjoyed a very thorny relationship, which got off to a bad start when Victoria launched into a chorus of 'Who let the dogs out?' when she saw Katie at the Manchester United VIP lounge. Katie retaliated by hinting darkly on *I'm A Celebrity...* that she knew various secrets about David, but that was all behind them now.

Indeed, in many ways, America was the perfect place for Katie to make her next moves. It is a country that encourages and rewards hard work, and, if there was one trait that she possessed, it was the ability to work hard. She was well aware of the potential there, too.

'I've got a drive: I am very ambitious for me and my children, I want to make a success of everything I do, and America is the next step for me,' she said. 'I love England, so I would never leave completely, but there's this little voice in my head that keeps telling me to try and make it in the States. I had some really great meetings out there recently and I am hoping to land some parts on films. It's all very exciting.'

But so too was her love life. Katie might have been coy publicly, but, in private, she was over the moon, so besotted was she with her new man.

'I've never met a man as hot as this,' she confided to friends. 'He's the real man that I've been looking for – he has set me on fire! I've never been like this with a man before. I've been writing love texts to him all the time, I'm soppier and more romantic than ever before. I am sure he is going to be the next great love of my life.'

The word 'next' was telling. When she married Pete, Katie had thought their relationship would last forever, but it hadn't. Inevitably, this provoked some disillusionment: she hadn't had a lot of luck with men before Pete. Indeed, for someone who had made their name as a much sought-after glamour model, Katie's relationships with Teddy Sheringham, Gareth Gates, Gladiator Ace (aka Warren Furman), Dane Bowers and Dwight Yorke, the father of her first child, had not been particularly successful.

Her first serious relationship was with Ace: they got engaged, but it ended when he became too jealous of Katie's career. The next was with Dane: the two met in 1999, when 19-year-old Dane, singer with Another Level, met Katie, then 21, at London's Met Bar. For a while, this looked as if it was going to be the love affair that Katie so clearly hankered after. In fact, she actually became pregnant, but opted for an abortion.

This was to be another episode that revealed that Katie had a very much more fragile side than she usually let on. So distressed was she after the abortion that she took an overdose of prescription pills and had to be rushed to hospital. She denied point-blank, however, that it had been a suicide attempt.

'No, it was probably just to get his attention,' she said. 'Stupid. I don't recommend it to anyone, it doesn't get you anywhere.'

She and Dane did not make the grade as a couple, but their friendship endured. In a strange coincidence, shortly after the split with Pete, Dane crashed his car outside Katie's house at four in the morning: he had split up from his wife. There was a short and totally erroneous amount of speculation that he and Katie had got back together, but it was nothing of the sort.

After Dane came Manchester United player Dwight Yorke, the father of Katie's oldest child. They met in 2001, when she was 23 and he was 27, although it was never a really serious relationship. At the same time, he was pursuing the television presenter Gabrielle Richens.

If Katie might have been wondering what she had done to deserve this sort of behaviour from her men friends, then what happened next must have given her cause for despair. Almost simultaneously, she discovered that she was pregnant with Dwight's child and the footballer was pictured in a nightclub with Gabrielle. In fact, he learned about the pregnancy from members of the press and was so incredulous that he asked if they were joking. Katie, meanwhile, in the way that woman so often do, was blaming it on the other woman, and not her errant man.

'Gabrielle Richens is nothing but a cheap slut and she has no idea how serious my relationship with Dwight is,' she snarled. 'I am expecting his child in April and we had planned to raise it together. Now I have no idea what to think or what to do. I'm devastated!'

It was something of an unfair comment, though, as Gabrielle would not have known about the pregnancy, nor that the relationship between Dwight and Katie was more serious than she had thought.

Initially, she considered having an abortion, as she had done with Dane, but then she had second thoughts. 'I thought, You know what? I'm successful,

I've got money, it's not like I can't bring up a child,' she said, and so she went ahead.

But, when Harvey was born, he had all sorts of difficulties with his health, as well as an all but non-existent relationship with his biological father. Given the way Katie refused to bow under at any stage, however, and simply got on with the task of bringing up a child with serious health issues as a single mother, she earned considerable respect for herself.

Peter Andre must have seemed a veritable Prince Charming after that, especially when he brought up Harvey unconditionally as if he were his own son; so to accept that their relationship too was not going to work must have been very difficult. Katie would thus appear to be accepting that, happy as she was with Alex, their relationship, too, had a chance of going wrong: hence he was her 'next' big love, not the 'last' one, nor, indeed, the only one. Katie had been through the wringer and she might be forgiven for sometimes being a little insecure.

But, for now, she and Alex were happy. In the background, however, the issue of Marie refused to go away. Like Katie, she was a mother and, as time went on, she seemed to become more and more angry about how she had been treated. When she didn't speak out herself, friends did so on her behalf: clearly, she wasn't at all happy about the situation.

'They were childhood sweethearts, but Katie has been chasing him for a while and it looks like he has caved in,' said one friend. 'Marie had a feeling that something was going on after she found text messages on Alex's phone.

'Katie has known Alex for the past year after being introduced by a mutual friend. Alex reassured Marie they were only friends. I don't think Alex thought that he'd fall for her and who knows if he has? It could just be the novelty of it all.'

Certainly, Katie and Alex were hogging the limelight. Everywhere they went a phalanx of cameras moved in their wake. It was heady stuff indeed for someone like Alex, who craved the limelight and yet had been unable to make it on its own. And if Katie found this ironic, given that she had accused Pete of gaining exposure through his relationship with her, then she wasn't saying. Anyway, she was a bona fide star: whatever she did caused headlines, and many a lesser person has had their head turned by that.

And Katie was wealthy, too. 'Marie bought Alex aftershave, socks and a kickboxing game for his PlayStation for his birthday,' the friend continued.

'The latest we heard from Alex was that Jordan has bought him a car. No wonder his head has been turned – Marie can't compete with that. Marie feels humiliated, like she is the last person to know.'

Nor could Alex's former girlfriend compete with Katie's flamboyance. Towards the end of July, she treated herself to a new horsebox – a bright-pink one, decorated with her silver tiara insignia. In fact, her choice was to cause problems – it was so obvious that it was Katie who was driving up the road whenever she took the horses out. Even so, it displayed a certain sense of style. No wonder the horsey set were sometimes bemused: not only was her horsebox pink, but so too was much of her riding gear. Katie was not, after all, a woman who liked to do things by halves.

Then there was her habit of flying to LA on a regular basis to get her hair done, although, of course, this was also wrapped up in the rest of her work. 'I do, about every three months,' she proclaimed, when asked about her expensive habit. 'Fifteen grand the whole thing costs for my flights and my hair. But my new management are part of CAA, and they're out there, so I have meetings there and things. They do stuff worldwide and they said, "Is it only England you want to do?" And I said, "No, I'm happy to travel and do other things." They're not bullshitters!'

Nor was Katie exactly subtle in other ways. She certainly knew how to attract attention when she wanted to get it: she was pictured trying on wedding dresses in a Bond Street store. It was inconceivable she didn't know the photos would create quite a stir: as it was, they caused uproar.

When Katie was pictured through the windows of a shop trying on various gowns, the rumour mill ran wild. Could she and Alex really have got so serious, so fast? No matter that she was still technically married to Pete: what was going on here? On top of that, Princess was present, which led to another furore about how much the children understood what was going on, and whether Katie should be trying on wedding dresses in front of her daughter (who, let it not be forgotten, was just two years old and therefore wouldn't have the faintest idea what her mother was trying on). But the critics didn't mention that.

And, while she might now have a new man, the war of words with Pete certainly hadn't let up. The latest barbed remark was to accuse him of ending the marriage in order to publicise his new album. 'The only thing I question is that he has an album out soon, and, if it's all about me and him not getting on, how would he be promoting his album, if he was still happily married to me?' she asked. 'It feels like he was maybe waiting for an excuse to end it. He's not the same Pete I knew. I hope he finds happiness, which he said he didn't have with me.'

That was bordering on the wistful, actually, as was another comment on the subject of the split: 'I miss the little jibes. I don't have anyone to argue with, or just smelling him walk past with his aftershave. Things like that I miss, but it's fine. I'll just spray my perfume instead.'

For Katie to accuse him of destroying their relationship just so that he got publicity for the new album was going a little far, even for her, but the same consideration applied: she had been very badly hurt. All the bravado in the world can't really heal a broken heart, and, although Pete may have felt that Katie pushed him into leaving, that's not to say she really meant to do any such thing. On the contrary, when her guard occasionally slipped, she was obviously still devastated. But Katie was Katie: she put the past behind her and attempted to focus on the future instead.

Besides, she had a new man to fuss over now. The latest to emerge from Camp Katie was that she wanted to give Alex a £100,000 makeover, as the years of fighting had taken their toll. 'Alex has never been vain, but, since he's gone out with Kate, it's like he's a different person,' revealed a source close to the couple. 'Dozens of fights have taken their toll on his face, so Kate has told him he has to go to a Harley Street clinic. Alex wants to get it done because he has taken on a new agent and is setting his sights on moving to LA and getting into films.'

There was another irony: some observers now felt that she was trying to turn him into Pete. 'She liked Alex because he was rugged and made Peter look like a complete wimp,' said one. 'But now it's like she's trying to turn Alex into Peter by insisting he has the Hollywood treatment.'

In reality, Alex actually looked fine, and Katie liked the masculine edge to his appearance. Nor, if he did have any work done, would it have been Katie who had to push him into it: as Marie had already observed, and was about to do so again at much greater length, Alex was as aware of his appearance as anyone and determined, like Katie, to show only a highly groomed appearance to the world.

Meanwhile, Pete was watching proceedings with a mixture of concern and bemusement. At the beginning of August, he effortlessly maintained the high moral ground, winning a libel case against the *People* newspaper, which had wrongly linked him with the model Shira Jones, while he was still married to Katie. The article falsely alleged he had made advances to Shira, who strongly resembled Katie, in Mo*vida nightclub the previous December. It had appeared in May, the month Katie and Pete split up.

After the case, Pete read from a prepared statement. 'This story has led to a lot of speculation about whether I was faithful to my estranged wife, which even led her to mention it on a breakfast-television show last week,' he said, flanked by his brother Michael and his solicitor. 'I have never been unfaithful to my wife, not with this girl or with anyone else. I'm pleased that the *Sunday People* have now accepted that their story was untrue and hurtful to myself. When things are untrue, I have to take action. I've not only got an estranged wife, I've got kids as well.'

Implicit in that remark, of course, was that he would be prepared to take legal action towards anyone who said he behaved badly while still married to Katie, including Katie herself. He was also, in the subtlest way possible, firing a warning shot: Katie's allegations must not become too far-fetched, he was saying. While she might be intent on winning the public over to her side, there was a line that she should not cross. He was backing up his words with actions: often, in the course of the marriage, Pete had appeared henpecked. He certainly wasn't giving that impression now.

Pete had been a true and honourable husband, that was evident, but he, like everyone else, could scarcely comprehend the speed at which Katie's new relationship was now moving. Alex's ex, Marie, was equally furious and fuming away in the background in a manner that was shortly to explode, with the couple at the centre of it all. Meanwhile, Katie and Alex were impervious to the doubts.

Katie went on Radio 2 to chat to Steve Wright: 'I like a man with talent,' she said pointedly. 'They have to have some kind of drive. It's very unattractive for a man to be none of those things.'

She continued to emphasise that she was the wronged party, too. 'I never wanted to split up with him,' she said. 'The reasons he split up with me were so stupid – it was all to do with the Andrew [Gould] guy. It was us working together and that was a big issue for him. When anyone gets married, you have to change a bit to compromise, but there's changing someone and completely changing someone. I love him as the father of my children but, in the last two years, we had marriage counselling. It's as if a weight has been lifted off my shoulders now.'

The marriage counselling was another snippet of information that was relatively new to the public domain. Pete had been talking about it, too, but neither would be too specific as to the exact grievances they both aired. Katie's ongoing friendships with the horsey set were clearly a bone of contention, but that alone wouldn't have driven them apart. The famous picture, in which Katie was seen on a night out with a number of men, including Andrew Gould, but not Pete, had often been cited as a cause for the final break, but Pete had scoffed at that idea, saying he was hardly going to bring a marriage to an end on the back of one photo. In many ways, of course, the couple had put themselves under almost intolerable pressure: a marriage lived 24 hours a day in front of the camera's focus is never an easy one to maintain.

And so Katie was now explaining the situation again to Steve Wright. The programme might have been broadcast to an audience of millions, but there was little doubt that she had only one pair of ears in mind. The combination of wounded emotion and hurt pride was still making her lash out: Pete had left and now she wanted to prove to him and the world that she didn't care any more.

'She really knows how to rub Peter up the wrong

way – and this interview would have really rattled him,' remarked a friend. 'It's fair to say that there is no love lost. Katie was hurting after the split and didn't want to say anything, but now she feels it's time to speak out. It really is no holds barred – poor Pete should keep his head down.'

But 'poor Pete' needed to do nothing of the sort: public opinion was firmly on his side. Nor did that change when another of Alex's girlfriends, Danielle Sims, a kick-boxer, crawled out of the woodwork: the pair had split up two years previously, but she was perfectly happy to tell all. Again, it was ironic: Katie's fame was reflecting not just on her new man, but on all his ex-girlfriends, too.

'Jordan might have found her match because he's absolutely sex mad,' she said. 'It's all he can think of. There's no holds barred with Alex – he loves a bit of slap and tickle, and he is up for everything!' Quite how much of everything was shortly to emerge, but it was only hinted at here.

'Alex was into everything – toys, dressing up, daring sex, outdoor sex – the lot,' Danielle continued, and she was to be proved very right indeed. 'He's got a one-track mind. I've heard he likes to dominate, but will happily let the woman take the reins, too. And he loves big, fake boobs.'

Katie was certainly the woman for him in that case, as both of them were only too happy to admit.

Danielle, who remained on friendly terms with her ex, was also able to provide an insight into the relationship. 'They are besotted with each other,' she said. 'He can't stop bloody talking about her! He loves her big hair, tan and massive fake boobs. That's what he goes for – the Barbie Doll type. To be honest, I'm happy for them and hope it works out. I don't know Katie, but I'm sure I'll be seeing a lot more of her from what he's been saying.'

But that was not quite so certain: Katie liked to be the centre of attention and for her to have her new man's ex hovering near by was not even remotely her style.

But how was this really going to pan out? Of all the men in Katie's life, only Pete stood out head and shoulders as the good guy, and now she'd lost him. Was the relationship with Alex going to be serious or just a diversion? Did he have her best interests at heart, or just his own? It was impossible to say at that early stage, but a friend of Danielle's sounded a note of caution.

'Alex is a bit childlike – a bit like a 15-year-old brain in a grown man's body,' she revealed. 'He constantly wants looking after and mothering. That's what happened with Danielle and she got a bit fed up of it. Once the lust and the sex dies down, it's hard to see him and Jordan working – although from what I hear she does like ordering her men around.'

Of course, Katie already had quite enough mothering to do, with three children to look after, and a career on top of that. But, according to the friend, there was something else that she and Alex shared in common. 'He loves the limelight, like Jordan,' she said. 'He'll take any chance to get on the telly or be seen. I wouldn't be surprised if we see him on *Celebrity Big Brother* one of these days.'

Or Katie's reality-television show at least.

CHAPTER SIX
The Detonator

Despite their initial coyness about coming out as a couple, within weeks Katie and Alex were all but living together. Alex had left clothes at Katie's home, and it had even been claimed that Junior was aware that something was afoot, asking Alex, 'Why are you sleeping in Mummy's bed?'

A source close to the action gave an insider's view. 'Alex now follows Katie everywhere,' he said. 'Katie has spent a fortune on nice drinks and takeaways for them over the last few days. Other people in the house don't know what to do with themselves – it's so awkward having him there all the time. Junior talks to him and said, "Why are you sleeping in Mummy's bed?" He seemed confused.'

He wasn't the only one. Pete was becoming more livid by the day, and the pictures taken of Katie trying on wedding dresses (actually, they were for bridesmaids) were flipping him over the edge. Princess Tiaamii had been present at the time, and Pete was said to be incensed about that too: 'If Katie dares bring our daughter into this, I will seriously flip,' he is reputed to have told Katie's mother, Amy. 'I've kept quiet about what she is really like, but one more stunt like this and I won't be able to keep my mouth shut!'

Of slightly more concern, now that Alex was practically living with Katie, was the fact that the children still didn't know that their parents were no longer together. 'When I leave them with Katie, I just say that Daddy has to go to work so that I can buy them toys,' said Pete. 'And when Katie hands them over to me, I just tell them Mummy is working.'

But they must have known something was amiss. By now their parents had been living apart for three months, and they were obviously unable to ignore Alex's presence. Indeed, he was becoming an everyday part of their lives. Sol Gilbert gave an insight into it all, when he described how the children met Alex for the first time over a roast-chicken dinner cooked by Katie at her home. 'It was just Katie and

Alex, her children, me and my missus and another couple,' he said. 'I'm thrilled they have been getting on so well as Alex is one of my closest friends.'

But she still wasn't winning the popularity war. Flaunting her new relationship so openly was bad enough, but then Katie committed another crime in the eyes of the public: she let her fans down. In the midst of a national publicity tour to promote the novel *Sapphire*, she cancelled an appearance in Bournemouth at the very last minute. Although her reasons were perfectly valid, namely she needed an emergency dental operation, her fans, some of whom had queued for three hours to see her, were not amused. Her spokeswoman tried to calm matters down, to no avail.

'I handed Katie a piece of chewing gum and, just after she put it into her mouth, a veneer came out,' she said. 'She was in a lot of discomfort and we found a dentist who would open up especially to treat her. He had to give her a lot of anaesthetic and her face swelled. She could not face the general public looking like that.'

Nor was that the end of it. 'I am a little worried that she may have swine flu,' the spokeswoman continued. 'She has been feeling ill over the past couple of days and she is spending some time in bed today. Katie is absolutely gutted to have had to pull out of the book signing today. The signing has been rearranged for next week and she is determined to make it back to meet the fans.'

A spokesman for WH Smith, where the signing was to have been held, also explained what happened. 'There were loads of people who had turned up, with some queuing inside the building and some outside in the rain,' he said. 'People were all disappointed.'

This one really could not be said to have been Katie's fault – but, even so, given how Pete was winning the popularity war between the two of them, it didn't help.

With that, Katie and Alex flew to Marbella to spend some time together. Meanwhile Pete, who Katie continued to cite as being the instigator of the break-up, revealed that he was still finding it very difficult to adjust. He had lost over two stone since the split and remained worn down by it all.

'I keep thinking that I should be getting through this, but I can't get it out of my head,' he said. 'Everyone around me keeps telling me to snap out of it, but it's not that easy. Some days are good, some are still bad.' After a breakdown in the Ikea car park, 'I had to go home and, that night, I cried myself to sleep. It's something I haven't done since I was a kid, but it was the only way I knew to get through that pain.' It was easier for Katie, he said, to 'just move on. [But] I can't do that. Well, not yet anyway. I don't know how anyone can move on that quick. It makes me question whether I ever meant anything to her, if any of it was real.'

It was, of course, but what Pete was seeing was the extraordinary way in which Katie was able to switch into her alter ego, Jordan, and then back again. One minute she was the devoted wife and mother, the next the barely clad vixen about the town. As a self-defence mechanism, perhaps, she had well and truly stepped into her nightclubbing side, but it didn't make it any easier for Pete.

'I loved Katie Price, but she left the building a long time ago now,' he said sadly. 'I never liked Jordan and my feelings haven't changed. I don't even feel I know her any more.'

As for the recent cavorting – he didn't pull any punches there. 'It doesn't shock me any more,' he said. 'I guess it's acceptance of the situation. The only thing I'll say is that I think her behaviour in Ibiza was a disgrace and I meant that. It wouldn't surprise me if Jordan said she was pregnant or getting married again; the hurt has shifted now and it's getting easier, week by week – I'm hoping the divorce is sooner rather than later.'

He was certainly having a lot to deal with. Katie was hurling everything she could think of at him, alleging variously that Junior would cry when it was time to go and stay with Pete, that Pete had orchestrated the split to publicise his new record, that she'd still like to have another child with Pete... It was bewildering, and clearly Pete thought so too.

'I really don't know how to react to comments like this any more,' he said (of the Junior remark). 'Kate has been putting me down for five and half years and it's a real shame she doesn't see fit to stop it now we're not even together. She makes jibes at me constantly and it really upsets me that she uses the kids to do it.'

As for having more children – 'Her comment about us having more kids together made me laugh out loud,' said Pete. 'As much as I love and adore the children we have together, there's no way I'd ever have any more with Kate. We are not together! Kate basically implied that I have orchestrated the whole thing. Can I just say that you'd have to be pretty sick in the head to end your marriage just to sell records! As if I would ever do something like that.'

Pete, in his own way, was attempting to move on,

too. He was filming a special called *Going It Alone*, and had also signed up to give a talk at the Edinburgh International Television Festival in August 2009. Katie, meanwhile, was in full Jordan mode, going a little over the top even by her own standards. She was pictured with Alex on holiday in Marbella, and the two put on a display of attention-seeking affection that really did almost go too far. It happened during an outdoor massage, when Alex persuaded the masseuse to move aside. 'Katie was getting a rubdown by a pretty female masseur when Alex sneaked up and started touching her behind,' said an onlooker. 'Initially, she didn't react, assuming it was the masseur getting a little overexcited. When his fingers continued to creep, she eventually looked up, shocked. When she realised it was Alex being slimy, she laughed raucously. Afterwards, they were giving each other an intimate rubdown with massage oil – it was pretty steamy, to say the least.'

It was shades of Ibiza all over again, although at least this time Katie was in a proper relationship with the man with whom she was cavorting. Clearly, she was intent on having fun, although not everyone was thrilled by it all. 'They were having a whale of a time, dipping in and out of the pool and generally larking around,' remarked an observer. 'They seemed oblivious to Katie's friends, who are staying in the villa as well, as they cuddled up together in the sunshine. It is a massive kick in the teeth for Peter, who has pledged not to have a new lover until the divorce is finalised.'

But she didn't care. The couple were having a whale of a time on holiday and, as ever, Katie was beginning to see a commercial possibility in her new life. Cage fighting had been a specialist sport to the extent that many people had not even heard of it a month previously; now, thanks to all the publicity Katie and Alex were generating together, everyone knew what it was. Could this be put to some good use?

'Cage-fighting bosses have been in touch with Katie's people to see if they can help them out,' a source commented. 'They believe the relationship between Alex and Katie will make the sport more popular and see people flocking to watch it. Talks went well and it's highly likely Alex and Katie will be looked after by the same reps.'

Just in case anyone didn't get the message, Katie was pictured wearing a T-shirt that bore the legend 'Good Girl Gone Bad'.

Katie's actions – and especially that outdoor massage – had brought a hail of criticism. She responded, as she had taken to doing, on Twitter:

'While Pete has the children, I don't want to be sat at home on my own,' she grumbled. 'I'm only human. It seems whatever I do is wrong.' As for Alex, she was light-hearted: 'I'm not getting engaged,' she said. 'I'm just seeing someone and like spending time with him.'

But Team Pete felt very differently. To be putting on such brazen displays when she was still a married woman was pushing it to the limit and there was heavy criticism from those around her ex. 'She really has no class whatsoever,' said one. 'She is just revelling in all the attention and knows it will just wind Pete up.'

In fact, *everything* was winding Pete up. The actual divorce now drew nearer and any number of fiddly little details still had to be finalised, including, bizarrely, custody of the two bulldogs, Pepsi and Hugo. Other items still in Katie's possession that Pete wanted back included kitchen utensils (he was a passionate cook), gym equipment and even his piano.

'Although he [Pete] got back most of his clothes and recording equipment, Katie still has the two dogs. She bought the girl dog, Pepsi, for Peter for Christmas, a few years ago, so obviously he has a special bond with her. But he wants to have both pets – he loves them to pieces.'

As for the rest of it – 'Secondary to his music,

cooking is Pete's other great love and he has asked Katie for some of the state-of-the-art kitchen equipment. He is really missing them and making do with items ad hoc at the moment. Their lawyers are currently wrangling over details of who gets what, but as yet they are still a long way from agreeing anything. It really is very awkward and increasingly hostile. The only thing keeping them both civil is the kids – they just want them to feel as settled as can be amidst all this upheaval.'

Of course, ultimately, expensive cooking equipment can be replaced, but the children were something else altogether and this was increasingly becoming a bone of contention, too. Although Katie and Pete were informally sharing custody, they were about to encounter the problem faced by every divorced couple: what to do about the kids at Christmas. Given how hard both had dug their heels in, it wasn't going to be an easy one to sort out.

'The kids are clearly devoted to their father and Pete feels he can offer them an incredibly stable Christmas,' said the source. 'He is not happy about the exposure Katie has been generating, cavorting topless and parading her new boyfriend around. He does not want a stranger looking after his kids. It is a serious bone of contention.'

Indeed, there was little in those days that wasn't and matters refused to calm down in the wake of an appearance that Pete made on Channel 4's *Alan Carr: Chatty Man*. The album, *Revelation*, was out and Pete was describing the accompanying single, 'Behind Closed Doors'.

'I'm a photographer,' he explained. 'I'm taking pictures, everything seems normal, but when I look back in my lab I'm thinking, Hang on, there's something different with these girls. It must be something wrong with my film. And then the woman ends up being an evil cow. Then, basically, she's possessed; she's trying to kill me. But deep inside, I know she loves me.'

Who might possibly have inspired that? The audience was pretty convinced. 'It was amazing,' said one observer. 'He was talking about the girl in the video, but we know that it's all based on what's happened in real life.'

Meanwhile, Katie was also using life to inspire art: out to promote her latest novel, *Sapphire*, she explained: 'The book is probably a bit what I am going through now. She [Sapphire] is going through a divorce, she's seeing a younger guy, she doesn't trust men, and she's got a boutique. She is just like me, really, but it ends up being happy.'

Which would imply that Katie herself was *not* happy and so, indeed, it seemed, although she did follow her remark by insisting hastily, 'I'm happy now, I'm very happy.'

But she simply couldn't seem to understand why the public appeared to be siding with Pete and not her: she had made her name in some ways falling, half-naked, out of nightclubs, but she wasn't able to understand that, as a wife and mother, the game had to change. All that near-naked cavorting with Alex in Marbella wasn't doing her any favours either, not at all. Meanwhile, decent, kind Pete, who was putting the children first and publicly pledging to stay single as long as he was legally married, was getting all the kudos.

Katie, who sometimes seemed to be permanently on the lash at that time, was getting none of the same acclaim. But the more the public disapproved, the more she appeared to revel in her behaviour – and then looked hurt when people said she should calm down.

'It seems like Jordan is going into meltdown at the moment,' said a worried member of her entourage. 'Things just aren't going her way and it's really getting her down. Peter seems to have upped the ante with his attack on her. He's really gone for the jugular and Katie has been completely taken aback by it all. It seems the public sympathy is all with Pete and Katie does not know which way to turn.'

Her spokesman felt the same way. 'It has upset Katie that she has been branded a disgrace by Pete,' he said. 'And it angers her that Peter feels it is OK to use the children as publicity to try and gain public popularity.'

In actual fact, they seemed as bad as each other when it came to the publicity stakes, with each doing everything they could to win the popularity war.

Pete, meanwhile, had settled down in his new place where, like much of the rest of the country, his neighbours were keen to show him solidarity.

'These lovely neighbours have been unbelievably kind, like leaving lasagnes or little things for me outside the door, and saying, "Don't worry, sweetie, mummy will look after you," which is really nice,' he told Alan Carr. 'It has been amazing because me and my brother Mike, we're like, "My God, we haven't been grocery shopping for two weeks!" The neighbours have been amazing, but now they're going to get tired of it, so I'm going to have to start giving food back, so I'm trying to find out what everyone likes.'

But the bone of contention between Katie and Pete

that just would not go away was the children. On the one hand, Pete was angry that they were already being exposed to Alex and, on the other, Katie was viewing Pete's frequent days out with them with a jaundiced eye. But then she was the one losing the publicity war – and that clearly rankled.

'I just want Pete to stop bringing our children into the divorce – that's between me and him,' she said. 'It's like he is trying to manipulate the situation to make me look bad all of the time. I could have responded in the same way because there's a lot of things I could throw back at him, but I haven't. I don't want to because I don't want to stoop to his level. My priority is to keep my children out of this and make sure they are happy. They have been through a big change recently; they should be being shielded from this, not being dragged into it.'

Nor was she very pleased about the fact that Chantelle Houghton had been invited to Princess's birthday party. 'I was not happy,' said Katie. 'I have kept my mouth shut on this for a couple of weeks, but it has upset me. She doesn't even know my children so I cannot understand why she is at the party. The kids have been introduced to her and then Pete dares to have a pop at me for them meeting Alex.

'None of this is fair – he is turning everyone

against me. I seem to be the bad one in all of this, but he walked out, he ended this marriage. I am tough, but there's only so much I can take – and I've had enough!'

Given the bitterness intensifying between them, Pete was not about to take this lying down. He had gone to Cyprus for a short break, but his spokesman had something to say on his behalf. 'Pete is genuine with his children, he only spoke about them because he was asked about a story that had appeared previously,' he said. 'He adores the children and takes them out to do things they want to do. He doesn't ask for the attention they get from photographers. As for Chantelle, she was invited to the party because she belongs to the same management company as Pete and there were lots of other friends there, and lots of children.'

But Pete had been stung by the criticism and he now wanted to go on record to set matters straight. Amazingly, he confessed that, in the early days of the separation, he would have considered reconciliation with Katie – but he certainly wouldn't now.

'If you had asked me a while ago if I'd go back then I would have kept my head low and dodged the question,' he said. 'But now I know I'll never, ever go back. I am over it, so, so over it – 100 per cent. I didn't think I'd move on this quickly, I thought it would take years, but I've finally accepted our marriage is over. I've shed my last tear. In everything there has to be an end point and for me this is it, I've reached it. It's been nearly four months, but I'm now in the light at the end of the tunnel.'

Although it was not always easy to get to the bottom of who really thought what as the war continued between them, it was, however, clear that Katie had been both devastated when Pete walked out and desperate to have him back. Now it seemed that it was her very public, very bad behaviour that had put an end to any hopes of that.

'Nothing about her can shock me any more,' said Pete. 'Nothing. When I walk down the street, I expect someone to tell me something shocking about her or something new she's said or done. Everyone around me is always shocked, but I'm not. For the first time it doesn't make me mad or upset; it simply washes over me. Once it would have hurt me so, so much, but not now.

'I've never said or felt that before. For three months, people have seen me crying and hurt, and going through all that. I was suffering – down one minute and happy the next. But whatever happens can't hurt me any more. Of course it's sad – it's the break-up of a marriage, but I've finally turned the corner and I'm ready to move on with my life.'

It also seemed that there had been a total breakdown in communication between the two. Now, their only way of talking to one another was through their legal teams – anything else was out.

'We haven't been in touch for over three weeks,' admitted Pete. 'All our communication now is done through lawyers. I'm not bothered who Kate dates, or who she's in a relationship with, as long as it doesn't affect my children. Unlike Kate, I'm not going to have a divorce party, but good luck to her!'

However, he reiterated that, because of the children, he was planning on staying single just for now. 'Throughout our marriage, I was completely and utterly faithful,' he said. 'When we split, I promised myself I would remain faithful. I have kept to this celibacy vow and will do so until the day our divorce is made official. I think I've proved it to myself and I'm happy. I know I can look back at this in years to come and feel I did the right thing and acted in the right way.

'You've got to think long term and think of the kids, which is what I've tried to do. I don't want them growing up and reading about things I got up to after splitting from their mum. Unfortunately, I cannot control what other people do.'

One thing that particularly irked him was Katie's reaction to pictures taken of him strawberry picking with the children in Worthing, West Sussex. She had publicly poked fun at him, writing on Twitter: 'Strawberry picking – what next?'

It was hard to imagine Katie out strawberry picking (although days out in the park with Alex were to come, sparking yet more negative comment), but it was one of the simple pleasures that Pete wanted to share with the children and he was livid at what she'd said.

'That's offensive,' he said, rather more sharply than he usually spoke about his ex. 'I'm trying not to react to anything she says, but I urge anyone to look over the last six series [of their reality shows] spanning five years and see how hands-on I've always been with the kids. I've been consistent with all three of them, whether there are photographers documenting it or not. I'm not going to stop taking the kids to do what they want to do, or give them the lifestyle that they deserve. We had a great day strawberry picking, although it turned out to be blackberrying as we missed strawberry season.'

There had been a reason for picking that particular pastime, too. 'I read Princess a bedtime story every night about a strawberry barbecue, so it meant a lot to her,' Pete explained. 'These are the things kids love doing. It's quite simple – kids need stimulation and need looking after. I feel I've said all I will say about the situation and I've put the record straight.

'After this, I don't want to say any more. I am over talking about her. That's not to say I won't retaliate, if provoked. If there's something that comes out that's bad, I may have to come out and retaliate to protect myself or my kids: I'm a parent and I'm not going to let things be said that will affect my children.'

One positive to come out of it all was that Pete's music meant more to him than ever before. Some years back, his musical career had been all but over, but now it was flourishing again, and Pete was loving what he was doing.

'For the first time in my career, I'm proud of my music and of this album,' he said. 'Natalie Imbruglia and Alesha Dixon have listened to it and congratulated me. Stuff like that means a lot. I'm looking forward in every way. I want my kids to have a happy life, with a mum and dad who love them. I look forward now and can see all these things in my life that I could never see before. Finally, I'm happy.'

But Katie's state of mind was more difficult to judge. She and Alex were now back in the UK – Katie made her way into the country wearing a very short, tight, fitted yellow mini-dress – and certainly seemed to be getting closer than ever. And Pete, while still attempting to refrain from criticising Katie, was publicly outraged when he heard that Junior might have seen the two in bed together.

'I heard Junior had been asking why Mummy was in bed with another man,' he said. 'I didn't believe it – I just thought it was kids saying things – but Junior has said it to me since. It's something a four-year-old should not be saying. I can't even bring myself to say the other name, but Junior just said, "Why is he in bed with Mummy? What is he doing in Mummy's bed?" That's the most disgraceful thing I have ever heard – ever!'

Katie denied point-blank that Junior had seen anything untoward, but it was yet another black mark against her in the public eye. Pete was winning hands down: he had all the public sympathy, and Katie's wildness just seemed to provide further justification for him walking out.

He was also making no bones about the end of their marriage: 'I don't miss her one bit!' he declared. 'I do miss what my parents have got – a good solid relationship. They have been married 55 years. I hated failing in marriage, that's what killed me as well as hurting the kids; I never wanted to get to that stage where I had to leave. Being a parent means everything to me.'

Of course, it meant everything to Katie, too – she just wasn't showing it so well. But this was nothing compared to what was to follow, for the two just seemed to grow in animosity towards one another, lashing out at every opportunity. By now, it was well and truly war.

CHAPTER SEVEN

An Affair To Remember

It was official: Katie was now definitely with Alex, while Pete maintained a very jaundiced eye on things from the sidelines. What was not clear, however, was quite how serious this new relationship was going to be. It had been a whirlwind: first, the split from Pete, then the drunken antics in Ibiza and now, a mere four months after parting from her husband, Katie appeared to be firmly ensconced with someone else. Or was she?

By this stage, she might be forgiven for barely knowing who she was. Katie or Jordan? Distraught wife facing a divorce she didn't want or wild cat, out to play on the town? Mother or model? Both, or were these two separate roles she could slide into at will?

Ever since she had first achieved fame as a glamour model over a decade earlier, Katie had become adept at putting forward any number of different images, retaining the ability to surprise and keep her public in thrall. But, even by her own standards, events were moving so fast that it was becoming increasingly difficult to stay in control of things.

Barely three weeks into the new relationship, the papers were full of conflicting reports about the state of play. One had it that – ironically, in the circumstances – Katie was worried that Alex would cash in on the relationship by selling his story. 'He's been getting on my tits,' she is reported to have said. 'I'm sick of him acting like a lapdog. He's been a distraction and he was fun while he lasted, but he's not good for me and now I feel ready to move on.'

Others had a very different take on it, with claims that she was even thinking of having a child with her new man. 'Kate is desperate for a baby and thinks that it will bring her and Alex closer,' said a source close to the couple. 'She feels she has a special bond with him. And now she knows there's no going back to Pete, she is determined to move on and put the past behind her. She thinks it would be good to start trying for a baby with him as soon as her divorce is finalised.'

The truth is that Katie herself most probably didn't know what she wanted. Events were moving too fast for her even to have time to think and, whatever she said in public, reports continued to circulate that, at the bottom of it all, she still wanted Pete. But she was right: that was no longer an option. If there had been a chance of reconciliation at the beginning of it all, there certainly wasn't now. Too much had been said, there was too much bitterness and harshness for the two to go back to being as they had been before. This most publicly lived relationship really was at an end.

There were also signs that Katie had been hurt by Pete's very open criticism of her recent behaviour, especially the claim, hotly denied by Team Katie, that she had allowed Junior to see her in bed with her new man. That fuelled suspicion that she might be ready to bring matters with Alex to an end.

'She's been stung by Peter's criticism and wants to try to focus on being a mum and trying to protect her reputation from any more blows,' revealed a friend. 'This has always been about companionship for her, not a serious relationship, but it quickly escalated. She wanted to end it in Marbella and is worried Alex has started to get stars – and pound signs – in his eyes.'

But then, should she have been so surprised? One of the reasons why Katie was so very good at what she did, and was able to stand out from all the other girls in the glamour/celebrity scene, was that, in her case, people were not just interested in her appearance alone: they were totally fascinated by her life. Katie had shown a canny ability to realise this and play up to it: all the interviews about her personal circumstances, the reality TV shows – she had turned her life into her art. Katie understood that, in some ways, her life had become a product; that was why people were so fascinated by her but it was also why it was so ironic that she may have been concerned that other people, specifically Alex, would be having the same idea, too.

So, was Alex enjoying all the attention? For a man who had been trying, with only a limited degree of success, to break through into the limelight, the answer was almost certainly yes. But then – so did his new girlfriend. Whatever her concerns about the relationship, Katie, of all people, would be able to understand how someone could see an opportunity in the lights of the media and use this to extend their career.

And, despite all the carping, the relationship continued – for now. Indeed, they engaged in family activities, Katie, the children and her new man, all larking about as if there wasn't a care in the world.

The couple were pictured playing with the children, flying kites and playing tennis while Alex swept a giggling Junior into the air. All three boys – Alex, Harvey and Junior, were bare-chested – to anyone who didn't know the background to what was going on, this could have been a regular family scene. But, if Katie was hoping that this display of unity, and the fact that Alex was plainly prepared to show that he got on well with her sons, would silence the critics, then she was wrong. It was too much, too soon and too fast.

And it did not calm the critics, who still seemed to feel that it was far too early for them to start playing happy families, something that was clearly very much on Katie's mind.

'I am trying so hard to help keep the routine of the children going through this period to ensure they are not affected in any way,' she said. 'I hear people say I am a bad mother as I never spend time with the children. I spend plenty with them, just not in public. While Pete has the children, he does what he wishes to do with them and I keep myself busy with work, seeing friends and having breaks overseas. I have to keep myself busy, otherwise I will go nuts.'

Pete, predictably, was horrified, not least because some of the pictures showed Katie and Alex engaged in a passionate embrace while the children were near by. He didn't say anything publicly, but a friend spoke out on his behalf. 'He is more upset than I have seen him since he left Kate – this really is his worst day,' the source said. 'He couldn't believe it when he saw the photos of his kids being fathered by this man he has never even met. For Kate to introduce this man into their kids' lives after just a few weeks is hard enough, but behaving like a pair of teenagers so soon after their dad leaves is another thing altogether.'

It seemed like something of a misjudgement on her part. And, although it might have helped her to deal with her feelings of rejection to have another man on her arm so quickly, while Pete remained resolutely single, Katie just didn't seem to understand that this was not how it played out to everyone else. After all, the children were still very young. How were they supposed to comprehend what was going on?

Not that she really could work this out. In many ways, Katie was actually in a state of shock. It still hadn't quite sunk in that her marriage was over, despite all the public bravado, and in many ways she still couldn't quite believe what had actually happened. Indeed, she hadn't been able to take it seriously at first.

'When Peter insisted that it really was over, she thought he was playing a joke,' said a friend. 'She honestly thought he was just kidding. They'd always had a fiery relationship, but they always kissed and made up. It wasn't unusual for them to go without speaking for two days or more after a row; Katie just presumed it would blow over, like it normally did. Despite trying to tough it out in public and saying she's moved on, underneath it, she's still in shock: she really loved Peter and wanted their marriage to be for keeps.'

That might have been behind a rare moment of warmth between the two. Pete's new record was out and Katie very briefly suspended hostilities to wish him luck. 'I really hope Pete's album and songs are a success,' she said. 'I know he has worked terribly hard on it over the past six months or so, and I know it means so much for him for it to work. He really does deserve that.'

But it was not to last: shortly afterwards, the two were back trading insults. Neither was prepared to back down.

As for Katie's behaviour, although it had raised eyebrows and angered Pete, others saw it for what it really was: a way of dealing with the pain she had suffered.

'This isn't the real Katie,' said a friend. 'This is her way of coping with the hurt.' Indeed, the frenetic way in which she was throwing herself from one activity to the next – and into a new relationship so soon – did rather suggest that she didn't want to allow herself a second to think. To have done so would have been to admit how upset she was and Katie simply didn't want to have to deal with that.

There was another indication of this in an interview she gave, in which she was required to provide short, one-off answers, as in: 'What would be your fancy dress of choice?' 'A pumpkin.' 'What is the worst thing anyone's said to you?' 'That I'm a bad mum and out-of-control.' 'Who or what is the greatest love of your life?' 'Pete was the love of my life.'

The last was extremely telling. It was clear that, whatever her protestations to the contrary, Katie had been very badly hurt. But what was also clear was that she simply hadn't understood how the constant bickering had begun to grate on Pete. He genuinely was a gentler soul than Katie and he had clearly wanted the type of marriage in which both partners were supportive of one another, led a quiet life and built up a stable family unit. Katie was eager for drama and passion, and didn't understand how weary this could make some people. And then there was the competitive aspect, the fact that she felt she always had to come out on top.

But this clash of egos, expectations and desires made for compulsive viewing and interest in the duo showed no sign of waning. The public continued to be fascinated by the state of affairs, although Pete himself didn't think it could last.

'People will get sick of it – *I'm* sick of it,' he said in an interview on the BBC. 'I think I have said everything I have had to say, I really do. I think enough is enough, and I just want to get on with it. It's become messy; it's become very public. I do want it to get to a point where we can just move on. [But] I can't blame anyone but ourselves – this is the life that we chose, you can't switch it off and on.'

They certainly couldn't do that. Although Katie and Pete were no longer together, their situation in some ways resembled a love triangle, with massive hostility between the two men, and Pete made no secret of his disdain for Alex. The new relationship, meanwhile, soldiered on. Katie was not exactly torn between the two of them, not least because one had walked out on her, but she certainly represented a figure in the middle. Pete and Alex were also beginning to represent opposite extremes: Pete the family man, who wanted nothing more than a happy home life and Alex the cage fighter, ambitious and determined to make it in the end.

Nothing was calm, everything forming the basis for yet more controversy. A fresh row blew up when Pete flew to Hong Kong in June to perform at the prestigious International Indian Film Academy Awards (IIFA) and proceedings were captured on camera by the crew filming his latest reality-TV show. Katie rang ostensibly to allow the children to speak to him, but almost immediately she began laying into Claire Powell. Claire was to feature increasingly heavily as the couple's fights wore on: she was the manager who had transformed Katie's image from vixen Jordan to loving mum and wife; she no longer represented Katie, but she still had Pete on her books. And she was the subject of Katie's wrath: Katie yelled that she was a 'fat, ugly, evil c**t'.

As events continued to unfold, it appeared that Team Pete was continuing to beat Team Katie – and Katie herself really couldn't believe how it was all playing out. The public had been in the palm of her hand for so long: why not now? And, of course, it was a vicious circle: the more upset she got, the more she lashed out.

Nor was Katie allowing herself to be comforted by those who could be counted on to have her real interests at heart. She had a slightly distant relationship with her father, Ray Infield, who had walked out on the family when Katie was four (many blamed this for her insecurities later in life), but, while the two were not close, Ray still had her best interests at heart. He got in touch with Katie once he heard about the split, but his attempts to offer solace were turned down.

'Ray sent Katie a text as soon as he heard about her split with Peter,' said Katie's former stepmother Shay, for whom Ray had left the family (the two had two daughters, but he subsequently left her, too). 'He wanted to check she was all right, like any father would. That was in May and he has still not heard back.

'Sporadically, he does try to get in touch and build a relationship with Katie, but she is so stubborn, she never replies. She is the same now that she was when she was a little girl: Katie gets what Katie wants. It's very sad. She always ignores his texts. Ray still cares, like any father. She is his daughter and he wants to be there for her. The problem is, Katie seems to be able to drop people just like that.'

But it may well have been this relationship that was at the root of all her problems. Katie had been left by Pete: she had also been abandoned by her father when she was only four, so perhaps, if she did have an ability to drop people, this might well have been self-protection. Ray had once hurt Katie very badly; it didn't take an amateur psychologist to see that she was determined he would never do this again. But then she had also been recently hurt, and her mood was turning increasingly ugly. Could it have been that Pete's departure had triggered an emotional response formed by the actions of her father when she was only four?

However, that's not to say that Katie herself hadn't played a huge part in what had happened in her most important relationship as an adult. Clearly, she had been difficult to live with and no amount of sympathy for her childhood trauma could cancel that out. She may have been damaged, and this had had a negative effect. In mid-August, there was another groundswell of public sympathy for Pete when a 90-minute TV special was aired, which showed the circumstances of his break-up with Katie. It dated back to the early days of the split, and showed Pete looking totally desolate and at an exceedingly low ebb as he shopped in Ikea for furniture for his new home in Brighton.

'It's obviously been four weeks since Katie and I split, and I'm out and about, trying to get stuff for the new house,' he said rather miserably, as he pulled up outside the store. 'I've found a beautiful home for the kids. Half my stuff is still in the marital home, so I'll just get some stuff in the meantime. My head's not in the right place, but I'll just focus on what I have to do.'

With that, he made his way into the shop, looking more miserable still. 'I've honestly never felt so low in my life,' he continued. 'Ever. I know it's a month gone, and I know there's people saying, snap out of it and you left her, so why are you feeling this? Thing is, nobody knows why I left her. I know why I left her. And, if people knew, they'd understand why I'm so upset. People handle things differently. Some people go out and party when they break up, not mentioning any names, but me? I'm just trying to deal with it the best I can for the sake of the kids.'

A deepening bitterness between the couple was also becoming increasingly apparent. The show filmed Princess Tiaamii's second birthday party, but, while she and Junior appeared on film, Harvey did not. This was because Katie didn't allow it: Pete could film Junior and Princess as much as he liked, of course, because they were his children, but Harvey was not his biological son – 'Guests are arriving, including Harvey, but his mother has refused permission for him to be filmed.'

Behind the scenes, things were getting more acrimonious still, with heavy, last-minute editing to make up for the lost footage. 'There's three months' worth of filming gone into making this,' said a source. 'Loads of it had scenes featuring Peter and Harvey together. It's been a nightmare learning so late on that we've had to remove so much from the film. We'll be working around the clock, trying to re-edit the show.'

Katie herself remained aloof. 'Sometimes, due to his illness, Harvey does things that Katie would not want people to see on telly,' said her spokesman. 'If he is with her, she's in control of what happens.'

Another source, however, revealed what was really going on. 'Katie's kids are turning into the real battleground of her divorce from Pete,' he said. 'With both of them having separate TV reality shows, the screen is becoming the place in which the custody battle is waged.'

That was true enough: indeed, it wouldn't be long before Team Pete and Team Katie started to judge which one was winning the popularity war by who got the most ratings. Katie also let it be known that she wished Pete to refer to her as Katie, not Jordan, on the grounds that it might come across as 'derogatory'. But, in truth, there was no area of life in which they were going to agree now. The insults continued to be hurled, the jibes made, the war fought... It was a very long way from the early days, when they had been so much in love.

At least Pete was able to feature the other children. He hosted another party on camera, this time for Junior's fourth birthday, during which he tried to explain how he was behaving in front of them, especially when he was feeling upset.

'I don't want these kids to be affected,' he said. 'I'm always laughing and smiling, and telling them Mummy loves them and it's important to spend time with Mummy. They shouldn't have to know what's going on. If Junior sees me upset, I just say I've hurt my foot or something. Princess doesn't understand anything, but Junior is very sensitive.'

Junior certainly seemed to know that something was going on. At one point, he appeared rather withdrawn and Pete did his best to try to cheer him up. 'You're so lucky, you've got so many homes,' he said. 'You've got England home, you've got the other England home, you've got Cyprus home, you've got Australia home. Daddy loves you and Mummy loves you, and Harvey loves you and Princess loves you. Who's your best friend?'

'Daddy,' said Junior.

'Thank you, mate,' said Pete.

There was an even more poignant moment when footage showed Pete in Macau, China. This was, of course, in the very early days, before feelings had soured so very deeply between the two, but Pete came across as wistful.

'I do miss her,' he said sadly. 'I hate missing her, I hate it. Funny thing is, I don't even know what I miss, because there was so much bad.'

But he didn't really miss her any more – that much was clear.

Sentiment for Katie continued to be negative: whatever she did, she just didn't seem to be able to win the public round. But then she didn't exactly help herself. Just as she had rounded on a fan in Ibiza, she did so again in August when her pink horsebox got stuck in a country lane. It must have been an exasperating occurrence, and it might have been annoying to be asked for an autograph when you are trying to manipulate a large vehicle in a small lane, but, even so, Katie didn't seem to realise that, every time she snapped at a member of the public, it reflected badly on her. It was another of the differences between herself and Pete: he came across as gentle and charming, whereas Katie could be extremely aggressive. And she often did herself no favours at all.

The woman concerned was a nursery nurse called Hannah McMullen, aged just 17, and the encounter took place in the New Forest, Hampshire. When Katie's horsebox got stuck, a group of onlookers gathered to gawp at her and Alex as she tried to manoeuvre the box.

'We were in our car and my dad suggested I got out to see if I could get a picture or an autograph,' said Hannah. 'So I did but, when I asked her, she said she'd run me over! It was the way she spoke. She was really stuck-up and sarcastic, and I'm not a fan at all any more. I prefer Peter Andre now.'

Her father, Simon, was also there. 'I always thought Jordan was a bit manky,' he said. 'My daughter, being 17, thought she was fantastic. We were driving along and watched this ghastly pink horsebox as it got stuck. My daughter went up to her for her autograph, but Jordan told her to get out of the way or she'd run her over. Jordan's boyfriend just sat there, picking his teeth.'

But Hannah wasn't the only one to be feeling more than a little miffed. Katie was also accused of making a racket at a nearby campsite, leading to still more upset. 'I was camping with my boyfriend and friends,' said Laura Smith, aged 18. 'In the morning, I went into the toilet block and heard people talking about how Katie was there. They were complaining about all the racket she was making – people had to keep telling her to be quiet. She was there with her boyfriend and friends. Apparently, she was being noisy after 11pm and people got annoyed. We saw them filming her TV show during the day and she did say hi to us when we waved.'

That was something, at least. Katie might have been lashing out because she was under so much stress, but she was lashing out at the wrong people. Those were her fans, or, at least, they had been and they wanted friendliness from their idol, not nuisance-making or the odd foul-mouthed barrage of insults.

Of course, the person her aggression was really directed towards was Pete. There had been a huge amount of speculation that he had fallen in love with Katie and ended up with Jordan, and even Katie herself appeared to confirm that at one point. 'I tried for five years to be something I suppose I wasn't really, just because I wanted the marriage to work,' she said. 'I was in love with Peter, but you end up rebelling.'

And now she was rebelling in spades but it was all so ugly that she was in danger of going much too far. 'I don't care if I ruin him,' she is said to have told one of her friends. 'I've told my lawyers that. I want to bring him down. I've lived a lie with him for so long.'

This was, however, the father of her children that she was talking about. A better tack might have been to try a more conciliatory approach, but it was too late for that.

Then there was the fact that problems had been brewing for years, so much so that the couple did make an attempt to sort out their differences before they went too far – but all to no avail. 'For the past two years, things weren't good,' said Katie. 'We had marriage counselling. And I really tried. I was never going to leave him because I believe you try and make things work. But now I'm not in that situation, it's as if a big weight has been lifted off. I think, Would I ever go back? There's just no way I could.'

The last was possibly a little disingenuous, for those reports that she was still besotted with Pete were refusing to go away. As she kept reminding everyone, it was he who had left, not her: she had never wanted the split. And none other than Alex was aware of that. 'I'm completely in love with her, but I do worry that our romance will end in an instant,' he told a friend. 'I shouldn't let paranoia overtake because things are great... most of the time. But the relationship has become so intense, so quickly, and I wonder if it's just too soon for Katie to rid herself of her deepest feelings for Pete.'

Almost certainly, that was the case; but invariably everything between them was not running smoothly. Katie and Alex were seen arguing on a night out, leading to speculation that their relationship was in trouble – and then they patched it up again. But it was so soon after the split with Pete, and somehow the public hadn't yet warmed to Alex in the way that they had done towards Katie's soon-to-be ex-husband. Katie and Pete utterly captured the public's imagination, while Katie and Alex were leaving them more than a little cold.

But interest in them remained as high as it had ever been. Katie's massive mood swings, lurching from criticising Pete to wondering how she could live without him ensured she was constantly in the limelight. Pete's innate decency, meanwhile, continued to shine through. Some bemused observers commented that the traditional male and female roles had been reversed, as it was Katie out on the town going mad, while Pete stayed home and looked after the children, but in truth it wasn't even as simple as that.

The real problem was that the two were incompatible, added to which Katie's intensely competitive streak encouraged her to see her husband as a rival, not someone on whom she could depend. She wanted to go wild and party; he preferred a quiet life, staying at home. In the first rush of love and lust, when they'd met all those years previously in the Australian jungle, it hadn't mattered so much, but then in the cold light of day, living their lives and trying to bring up a family, it was more of an issue.

And matters were about to intensify still more.

CHAPTER EIGHT

A War of Words

As time wore on, matters between Katie and Pete didn't get any calmer: quite the opposite, in fact. The arrival of Alex on the scene had complicated things considerably, not least because it was no longer just a case of Katie having a new man. Alex appeared to be assuming, to some extent, the role of father to the children and, while Pete might have been able to countenance his estranged wife finding another lover so quickly, he was finding it considerably more difficult to relinquish any degree of his paternal responsibilities to another man.

Indeed, in many ways, this undermined what Pete's entire life had been about. He'd had a degree of success with his music, but he was never going to be one of the all-time musical greats, and he knew it. What he was exceptionally good at, though, was being a father, and that meant the world to him. He adored the children and they adored him, and to have to see them with another man so soon hurt him considerably. Even worse was witnessing Katie and Alex indulging in such physical displays of affection with the children near by: this was something they wouldn't have been able to understand and, for Pete, it was particularly hard to bear.

Things came to a head during the course of another phone call: Pete was still angry about the pictures of Katie and Alex frolicking with the children near by, and became even more so when Alex became a part of it all. The children were with Pete when Katie rang to talk to them: she then put Alex on the phone to talk to Junior. Pete was absolutely livid.

'Peter was outraged,' said a source. 'He was screaming at Katie, saying, "He's not the father of my children!" Katie couldn't believe it. One minute she was chatting to Junior, and the next Peter was on the line, incandescent with rage. He started accusing her of completely inappropriate behaviour by frolicking with Alex in public in front of the kids. He hated the pictures of Junior playing with Alex, saying repeatedly that it "wasn't right".'

This was actually the first time the duo had spoken to each other for quite a while (they mainly used their lawyers now), which was perhaps why Katie hadn't quite taken on board how angry Pete had become. But he was beside himself, and had no qualms about showing it, too.

'His reaction really stunned Katie,' continued the source. 'She clearly didn't appreciate how he was feeling. She's desperately trying to move on with her life and it really set her back emotionally. She just wants to be happy and is sick of confrontation. Yes, it must be strange seeing another man with your kids, but she thought Peter could deal with the situation a bit better. Peter has always taken his responsibilities as a father very seriously, so she can see where the anger has come from.'

Indeed, Pete was becoming increasingly upset by the extent to which the children were being drawn into it all. They now knew that their parents were separated, but there was, at least, a chance that they might be shielded from the increasingly bitter fallout. However, the angry phone calls, and the fact that both were featuring on their parents' reality-TV shows, meant that they were seeing far more than they could understand or deal with, and Pete was feeling increasingly fraught.

'The kids come first for me, and if I see any of them upset or frightened, or scared, it gets me every time,' he said. 'It makes me feel sick to think they are scared or upset – it's not right. It's the one thing that can still hurt me. I don't want the children used. I want things to stay as normal as possible for them – Junior is already asking questions. I always want the kids to be safe and happy and feel loved, whoever is around them, and I want to protect them as much as possible. When they are with me, I will always ensure that.'

The trouble was, though, that, as long as their parents were incapable of being civil to one another, then the children would always be aware of the strains. Katie had an on/off friendship with Kerry Katona, and would have seen that, after Kerry's divorce from Brian McFadden, there was a breakdown in communications between the duo (who had two daughters) to such an extent that they didn't speak at all. Was it possible that the same thing would happen to her and Pete? It was in the interests of the children, after all, that some degree of communication was maintained, but, such was the bitterness and anger both were feeling, it sometimes appeared that they could either shout at one another or not speak at all. There was still no way the two could approach the situation with anything like a degree of calm.

Meanwhile, the ongoing war between the two took on a bizarre twist. An organisation called www.OnePoll.com carried out a survey of Twitter users and came to the conclusion that Katie was the most annoying celebrity Tweeter. 'Jordan's tweets are the worst ever,' said a spokesman. 'They are vile, unintelligent and bitter and have no purpose other than to bait her ex-husband. She has nothing whatsoever to say which appeals to anyone except herself. Peter Andre's tweets are as dull as dishwater, but at least they do not mention his very public split with Jordan.'

So, it was another victory for Pete – of sorts.

Katie attempted to rise above it. She and Alex went for a night out in the West End with her friends Gary Cockerill and Phil Turner (though they had once been friends with Pete, they now appeared firmly rooted in Team Katie), going to see *Priscilla, Queen of the Desert*, before moving on to dinner at The Ivy. Katie was looking spectacular: she donned a zebra-print dress for the occasion, heavy make-up and a very bouffant hairdo. The message was that she was doing just fine. Responding to the criticism of her relationship with Alex, she said, 'Pete's the one who broke up with me and it's good I'm moving on. I'm really happy with Alex.'

And so it went on. Pete was pictured taking the children on a boat trip, amid speculation that he might return to the celebrity jungle where he and Katie first met. Katie, meanwhile, started making plans for another trip to the Mediterranean, to Marbella, for the European launch of her equestrian range.

That aspect of her life, at least, was going according to plan. Observers had been concerned that the wildness of her recent lifestyle would damage her commercial interests, for Katie was not exactly behaving like a standard role model for young girls. But it hadn't proved to be the case. While there might have been a fair amount of disapproval voiced about her behaviour, public fascination was as strong as ever and opportunities kept coming up for ever more varied work. And there were plans to extend the brand, as it were, to a much more international audience than before: Katie was obviously planning a future that encompassed much more of the world than just Britain, hence the Marbella trip.

However, this time round, her advisers took a firm line and told her to be careful when it came to alcohol. The previous two trips, when she'd run wild in Ibiza and then again when she was pictured nearly naked with Alex in Marbella, had been public-relations disasters (to say nothing of the effect they might have on the divorce) and everyone involved was adamant that such a debacle wouldn't happen again. Although her image had not, as some worried, been damaged beyond repair, she wasn't doing herself any favours – and, as the divorce neared, issues surrounding custody of the children were beginning to make themselves felt.

'Her image took a battering on those two occasions and her people are desperate for this not to happen again,' revealed a source. 'The majority of her indiscretions arise as a result of her drinking. She readily admits that she becomes a different person when she drinks and she tends to lose control. She's got quite a petite figure as well, so her tolerance isn't the highest. This doesn't really help matters.'

Indeed, this was a business trip, not a pleasure outing. As well as the launch, Katie was due to attend a polo match and her team did not want business to be overshadowed by play. 'Her people want nothing to detract from the range – and, if she's not drinking, then they're on much safer ground,' continued the source. 'When it comes to her business, Katie is a true professional so she wouldn't want to be partying hard, anyway. But, in any case, she's very aware that image is very important – especially in the business world.'

That aspect of her personality had certainly not changed since the split with Pete. Whatever swings there might be between the Jordan/Katie aspects of her character, there was one constant: her business nous. In one of the final arguments the couple had before the split, which was captured on camera for all the world to see, she had, unkindly, brought it home to him that *she* was the person in the family who, to put it bluntly, made most of the money. But this was true. By this stage, Katie had amassed a fortune estimated to be about £30 million and she clearly had no intention whatsoever of cutting back on her career. Anyway, work took her mind off other things. As she herself had said, if she sat at home doing nothing, she'd go mad.

Not that she was the only one to fret about the effect that the split might have on her career. Pete, too, was concerned about the implications: '[I asked myself] what if, after this break-up, the public completely turn against [me]?' he asked. 'This could be the end for me.'

Indeed, with the launch of the single and the album coming up, Pete pointed out that leaving Katie was a huge gamble and certainly not the publicity stunt that some people were saying it was. In fact, the release was even delayed from early summer (when Pete actually left) to early autumn 2009, simply because of the turmoil in the rest of his life.

'We put the release back because of what happened,' he admitted. 'I told my manager this could have been the end for me. It would have been better to stay in the relationship.'

And then there was the fact that so much of the album had been inspired by what was happening in the marriage. Pete seemed to think that, if only Katie had taken an interest in what he was saying through his work, their problems might have been sorted out. 'I used to say to Kate, "Why don't you listen?"' he explained. 'These were my letters.'

As it was, he felt that he was telling his story through the new songs. 'Some of them say a lot,' he said, going on to muse about what a positive reaction he was getting from the fans, which was all the more remarkable, given the career he'd had in the mid-1990s had seemed to dry up.

'I never thought I'd get it back,' he confessed. 'But when things went weird in 1999 and I went away for three years, I used to pray, and say that. if I got it back, I'll never take it for granted again. I hid from the public [for the three years he was away]. That's the reason I'm so appreciative now. I'm not arrogant, I'm humble – I know it could all end.'

This time he was hoping that he could have a very different musical career from the first time around. 'If I keep bringing out music that's not too cheesy, too poppy, with credible lyrics; if I keep bringing out the right sort of things and people give me a chance, I could have a better career than I had before,' he mused. And he certainly wasn't arrogant, as became apparent when he was talking about himself. 'There's still a stigma to the name,' he said. 'Even *I* wouldn't play "Insania" in my own car!'

With an attitude like that, it was hardly surprising the public loved him more than ever.

And so both Katie and Pete were hard at work on their careers. Katie was pulling herself together in other ways, too. She and Alex had decided to take part in the New York Marathon and she was in training, which meant that she was also drinking less. (The fact that she'd recently run the London Marathon with Pete was not lost on anyone, nor that she intended to run the next London event with Alex.) She remained extremely thin, however, and there were fears that she was still so stressed out that she was finding it hard to manage a normal diet.

·'She's already cut back on the booze in light of the new exercise regime and is feeling great,' revealed a source. 'Alex is helping her with the training and they've both been taking it very seriously.

'It's very poignant that the two of them are doing it [the London Marathon] together – especially as Peter did the Marathon with her last year. It shows that she's completely moved on and is looking to the future with her and Alex. It's been tough, but she's starting to forget about Peter and all the heartache is slowly ebbing away.'

But she hadn't moved on, not really. That much was clear from the constant public sniping: if she and Pete had really been indifferent to one another, they simply would not have bothered any more. But neither could let up for a minute: if Katie wasn't flaunting her new boyfriend, then Pete was.branding her a bad mother, while both were hinting darkly, although never particularly revealingly, as to the real reasons why they had split up.

And there continued to be behind-the-scenes reports of Katie's ongoing love for Pete, whatever she might say in public, with accounts surfacing about frantic text messages and messages left on his answering machine. Nothing was as clear-cut as it seemed.

While the war between the two raged on, members

of the public were also taking sides. There had been quite a few raised eyebrows when pictures of Katie cavorting were made public (although far, far worse was to come) and sometimes that spilled out in public reactions, too. On the eve of the Marbella trip, a nasty incident occurred, when Katie and Alex had a night out at Brighton's La Tropicale club, followed by a kebab. A member of the public saw them and lashed out at Katie, so much so that the police had to be called.

'This woman came out of nowhere, shouting at Jordan, "You're a slag, you're a slag!"' said a witness. 'It was a really nasty scene. Alex got in the middle between Katie and the woman, but she just carried on shouting abuse at Jordan and telling her how much she hated her. Alex looked really frustrated while Katie just ignored the woman and pretended nothing was happening. She only left when Security came in from the nightclub next door and removed her.

'But as soon as they left, she returned, holding up a piece of paper saying, "You are a slag" next to the couple. Eventually, the police turned up and sent her on her way.'

For a woman more accustomed to adoration from the crowds, this must have been a truly unpleasant shock for Katie. And it also highlighted the danger of leading a life quite so publicly as she, Pete and now Alex, too, were doing. Because so much was on film, or talked about, or confessed to, or analysed endlessly in everyone's columns, when people met any of the three main protagonists of the drama, they tended to think that they actually knew them and could pass judgement in any way they liked.

Of course, no one was in full possession of the facts, but it meant there was a real danger of people lashing out, verbally or even physically. Katie had been out there since she was 17, and was well accustomed to provoking public reactions, but even she seemed taken aback at quite the depth of the passion this particular episode had unleashed.

Pete could only watch in despair. At least public opinion was well and truly on his side, and so was the celebrity community, too: there were reports that he had formed a friendship with Duncan Bannatyne, the Scottish entrepreneur and star of *Dragons' Den*, who was offering him moral support.

'Duncan has been a tower of strength,' revealed a source close to Pete. 'Like Peter, he's a family man and he understands. Peter has a particular bond with Duncan because he's a father too.'

Katie continued to be pictured with the children: she and Alex took them out for a day at a theme park.

Pete, meanwhile, made a short trip to Cyprus, looking more cheerful than he had done for some time: his single went into the charts No. 4, his reality-TV show attracted 1.7 million viewers and life was looking up. Despite the split, in many ways, this was a new lease of life for him: having lost and then recovered his career, he talked publicly about how grateful he was that that particular aspect of his life was back on track.

But nothing was ever quiet for long in the war between Katie and Pete. Indeed, it was soon to be the turn of someone else to step into the public eye. When it first became public that Katie and Pete were a couple, the name Marie Thornett came up. She and Alex had had a ten-year on/off relationship. Marie, 29, came from Aldershot, Hampshire, and had first started dating Alex in 1999: during a break in the relationship she had a son, now three, with another man. Until then, she had been quiet but, clearly, she had had enough and came out with a devastating account of what Alex was really like – although even this paled into insignificance in comparison with the revelations that were to come. She was obviously livid about what had been going on, withering in her put-downs and casting aspersions on what the real motives of her ex might be.

'Alex has only one real love – and that's himself,' she said. 'Fame and fortune are what drives him. We used to snuggle up and watch Katie and Peter Andre's TV show. He used to joke he'd get with her for the money and then come back to me. It's definitely not funny now. He's vain and vacuous. I believe they are made for each other.'

The problem seemed to be that Alex had done a spot of double parking: he hadn't quite got round to calling time with Marie before hooking up with Katie. Understandably, Marie, given the circumstances, was spitting tacks. Matters came to a head when she was forced to fly out to Majorca on her own, as Alex had said he was preparing for a big fight, only to discover that his plans were a little bit more fluid than she'd thought.

'We stayed in regular text contact through the week,' said Marie, who was clearly intent on letting everyone know exactly what had been going on. 'On July 18 he texted, saying how he wished he could be with me. It was only a few days later, when I got home, I discovered that was the day of Michelle Heaton's birthday party, where he first got it on with Jordan. That was so cruel of him.'

Indeed it was, although it certainly wasn't the first time that someone had been so impressed by a new lover that the switchover became a little messy. In this case, however, the very public nature of it all didn't help: Marie didn't just find out that Alex was seeing someone else, she saw pictures of it splashed all over the newspapers. Alex might have felt bad about it all, but his former girlfriend was having none of it.

'I couldn't believe it when he posted a message on his Facebook page saying, "Alex Reid has struck gold". He was talking about Jordan. That says it all about how crass he is.'

Then came those increasingly notorious snaps of Katie and Alex playing with the children in the park. Pete wasn't the only one to have got upset: Marie wasn't very happy either, and was only too keen to get the message across.

'Alex was always a bit of a groper,' she said. 'At family celebrations, he would be really cuddly, pulling me on to his lap and smacking my bum. He'd get me in the same snogging position he was in with Jordan in the park – on top, with his arms around me – even in front of my grandparents.

'And I laughed when I saw one of their first dates was at a theme park. He did exactly the same thing with me.'

It was all pretty hurtful stuff.

Alex certainly had an unusual way of introducing

himself to his new girlfriend's parents and this was something else that Marie was intent on drawing to the public's attention. 'He asked my mum to wax him – and she's not even a beautician,' she explained. 'I was there as well, and he took off his trousers and had a tiny G-string on. I've never forgotten it. Alex wanted the full works, but my mum drew the line at his legs. He hasn't got a single hair on his body – he waxes every inch of himself. Mum saw the funny side, luckily.'

Nor was this the only occasion when Alex put on a show of exhibitionist behaviour.

'Another time, on a hot summer's day we were in the back garden with my family, and out of the blue Alex asked us to turn our backs to him,' Marie continued. 'When we turned around, he was completely naked, pouring a bucket of water over his head. He didn't make a show of it: he just calmly put his shorts back on – he always goes commando. We were stunned.

'He's worse than any woman when it comes to beauty. He loves sun-beds. He's always in the garden, topping up his tan. And his nails are immaculate. He has mirrored wardrobes in his bedroom, there's a mirror on the wall and on the windowsill. But at night he wears a nasal strip to stop him snoring, and sometimes forgets to take it off.'

As if all that were not enough – more than enough,

really – Marie was also eager to disclose that the parts he played could be very seedy. 'My dad rang me late at night, saying, 'Turn over, Alex is on TV,' she recalled. 'I couldn't believe what I was seeing. He was playing someone who gets his kicks out of filming people having sex. He had gone out to work that night and hadn't mentioned a thing.'

Of course, it is all too easy to write these comments off as the fury of a woman scorned, but there was a poignant side to it, too. Readers would have been justified in wondering why, if Alex was so ghastly, Marie had canoodled with him on and off for a decade, but it turned out that, as Marie herself admitted, he had a very different side to him.

'But Alex was also an amazing guy,' she said rather wistfully, softening her tone considerably. 'He was a romantic and deeply sensitive. I believed, no matter what, that he loved me. On Mother's Day last year, he had flowers delivered to my son's nursery when I picked him up. He gave me love poems. If I had a really stressful day, he'd treat me to a takeaway or pay for a haircut. He'd rub my feet or massage my back, and he was a thoughtful lover. [But] before every fight, Alex insists on a ban on sex for at least a month. He says he has to be focused. I did support him, but at times that was very wearing.'

Perhaps unsurprisingly, Marie believed that Alex was with his new love because of what the relationship could do for him. For years, he'd been struggling to make it as an actor with little success, but now he was receiving the kind of attention most would-be thesps could only dream about.

'Jordan should be very cautious,' Marie continued. 'He might think he's in love, but he is also in love with the idea of being rich and famous. He used to mouth "I love you" [to Marie] when he was in the ring and he'd tell people in nightclubs I was "The One". Before Jordan, he was struggling to make it as an actor. Now he's playing the big man, mixing with celebrities, travelling the world and getting his picture in the papers.'

As for their own break-up – 'I'm not against him moving on, I just think there's ways in which this could have been done,' she admitted. 'And parading it in the public eye is not one of them. I have huge sympathy for Peter Andre. I hope he finds the strength I'm trying to find to move on.'

But if Katie and Alex were at all concerned, they didn't let on. Katie left her boyfriend at home for a rare night out by herself: accompanied by close friend Gary Cockerill, she went out to a birthday party for the comedian David Walliams. It was a celebrity-studded event, with the likes of Geri Halliwell, Kimberley Stewart and Matt Lucas also in attendance. This was Katie's metier and she looked as if she hadn't a care in the world.

Pete, meanwhile, was determined to do what was right by everyone. He had also gone public about the fact that he intended to look after his children. One of the lyrics in the new album addressed that as well: 'How can a man not want to claim his own, leaving a mother to raise her child alone?'

It had attracted the notice of others, too. 'Somebody pulled me up on it and she said, "Well, that means nothing now because you're not with your wife,"' he related. 'I said, "Hold on a second, I never left my kids!" I will never not raise those children – I'm claiming my own and I also want to claim him [Harvey] as well, if I'm allowed to, so, to me, the song makes even more sense because I would never leave a mother to raise a child alone, especially his own kids.'

His concern was palpable, and it shortly became a good deal more so, when Alex openly admitted to taking Class A drugs. 'I've done cocaine once too often, say like once every month or after a fight, and that's not good,' he revealed. 'It's not good for a fighter because it's taken vital years off my longevity in my health to come back.'

He also talked quite openly about some of the people he had worked with in the cage-fighting world, many of whom had a slightly *laissez-faire* attitude towards what was legal and what was not: 'They are good people just bending some rules,' he said.

But it was yet another worry for Pete: already he had been worried that a cage fighter was not an ideal father figure, but to learn that Alex would quite happily admit to drug-taking and mixing with somewhat dodgy people concerned him even more.

'As far as Peter is concerned, Reid is not an ideal father figure and shouldn't be responsible for another man's children,' said a friend, with commendable understatement. 'Now that he's admitted taking cocaine, it will send Peter through the roof knowing that this man is anywhere near his kids.'

All in all, it was an uncomfortable time for everyone. Pete was worried about the children, while there were also reports that Katie sometimes tired of Alex, but the relationship was now so public that she could hardly say so or admit to herself that she might have any concerns: that would have meant losing face, and, if there was one thing Katie never did, it was to lose face. And for all the problems, Alex took her mind off Pete: Katie liked having a man on her arm, was rarely without one and needed some moral support as she headed towards her divorce.

However, the storm about drug-taking, cage fighting and mixing with risky people was about to be totally overshadowed by what came next. At last, Alex was to star in a film, something that had been arranged well before he got together with Katie. He was hoping this would finally provide him with his big break, something he had been working towards for years. But the nature of the film, and the comments it would ultimately provoke from Katie, caused a huge row, both publicly and among intimates of the couple.

The break-up between Katie and Pete was bitter, uncomfortable and hostile. What's more, one sensational secret after another had been frequently exposed. However, all that was about to be placed in the shadows by the explosive revelations to come next.

CHAPTER NINE
Cage-fighting Man

The pictures, when they appeared, were sensationalist. There was Alex, Katie's new boyfriend, seemingly on the verge of strangling the young woman writhing underneath him. Given how much controversy Alex had attracted since hooking up with Katie, it seemed surprising that he would pose for such a picture – but he did.

It soon emerged that the brunette was the actress Yvette Rowland and the action was taking place on the set of *Killer Bitch*, a film starring Alex and Yvette. It was Alex's big break – for years, he had been desperate to get into movies with a proper starring role – and it was not, as was erroneously first reported, a porn flick. In fact, it was a crime tale, with

Alex as leading man. Unfortunately, the scene started off with the Alex character strangling the Yvette character, before the two got carried away.

'They were red-hot,' said an on-set source. 'Alex and Yvette came over brilliantly on camera. The sex scenes were crackling with intensity. You could have thought it was for real, if you didn't know the cameras were there.'

Filming was taking place at a historic mansion called Clock House in Capel, Surrey, and there were reports that Katie had forbidden excessive physical contact between the pair – very unlikely, given that Katie, of all people, knew what was required to court publicity. The pictures, however, were graphic and thoroughly unpleasant to many. Indeed, they made some observers believe that, after her summer of wildness, Katie was in danger of destroying her image for good. And, with the divorce now fast approaching, they could present massive problems for her.

'Katie's advisers have warned her that any unsavoury publicity connected to her could come back to haunt her in the divorce courts,' revealed a source. 'She knows Peter and his family don't particularly like Alex and his circle, especially now he's been introduced to the kids and is beginning to play a part in their lives. She wants to present a family-friendly image to the world, but believes shots of Alex romping with another woman, albeit for a film, could harm her chances.

'Katie wants Alex to be viewed as a suitable father figure, not some kind of B-movie porn-type star. She has visions of Andre's people throwing pictures of the scene in front of the divorce judge. It hardly reflects Alex as Mr Clean.'

It certainly wasn't your average family film. *Killer Bitch* was described by the makers as a 'fictional full-length feature with real fights, real criminals and real sex', in which Yvette 'takes part in a deadly game in which she has to kill five people or all her friends and family will be murdered'. Other participants included reformed gangster Dave Courtney, Mikey Carroll (best known as the 'Lottery Lout') and ex-soccer hooligans Jason Marriner and Cass Pennant. Mary Poppins, it wasn't.

Reports varied as to Katie's attitude to it all. 'Neither Alex or Yvette had any problems with stripping off, but, when he mentioned it to Katie, she flew off the handle at Alex, who just shrugged his shoulders,' said a source. 'He then ... just fobbed her off, telling his film bosses he'd still do the scene. He didn't want to let them down. After all, he signed up for the film long before he got together with Katie.'

It all became increasingly graphic, with a simulated rape scene that would soon enough cause more controversy when Katie came forward to defend her man. As it was, alarm in some quarters, not least Pete's, was going off the Richter scale. 'The pictures aren't pretty,' said a source. 'Kate was aware of the film and what it entailed, but seeing it for herself didn't go down well. It's very seedy. A number of friends and her media advisers feel her relationship with Alex will be detrimental to both her and her career; they desperately want her to leave him before it's too late.'

Pete, of course, was beside himself. He had never liked Alex from the start, but this would bring home to him just how different a man Alex was from himself, and quite how apart their values were. And as the father of young children, Pete's concern was doubly understandable: given how much the kids had already been exposed to, what might happen if they somehow saw these shots?

'Pete's beyond outraged by this new low,' said a friend. 'He thinks it's absolutely disgusting and can't believe his children are spending time in the presence of this man.'

Alex, however, was getting pretty angry too. Given this was supposed to be his big chance, his debut, to be spoken of as little more than a porn star was upsetting him so deeply that he was beginning to consider seeking legal advice.

'*Killer Bitch* is not a porn film, it is a gangster movie in which Alex is the main character,' said his spokesman. 'The rape scene has been taken completely out of context and Alex is speaking to lawyers.'

Despite all the speculation about Katie's reaction, she still hadn't said anything publicly about the new film, although she soon would. Instead, she was doing what she did best: adopting a totally defiant air and getting on with her life. Asked about her state of mind, she replied, 'What have I got to cry about? I have got a great life, great kids, I enjoy my horses. I can't complain, so I don't need to cry.

'I am not the only one that goes through divorce, it happens every day. I was clear in my head where I was going, there was no heartache to get over. I am a strong girl and I would advise every girl out there, if a man says it is over, don't go grovelling back. It is over, end of, move on! Pete made it very clear it was the end and he didn't want to go back. So what am I supposed to do, wait until he says I can have a boyfriend? I don't think so!'

And it was at that point that she really did herself proud. The reality cameras were, as ever, trailing her around, and so it was that Katie was able to deny rumours of a pregnancy by revealing that she had done a test with the cameras rolling. Even her most stalwart supporters thought this was going a little too far, but Katie was, as always, blithely unrepentant. It was her life: if she chose to reveal the most intimate details of it on live television, then why not?

'I am not even pregnant and you will see that on the show,' she announced to one startled reporter. 'I did a preggie test upstairs with the cameras. I let them come in the toilet and they watched it develop, and I said, "Does that look like I am pregnant?" I got the box and I thought, Let's prove it.

'I actually have one in my bag as well, 'cos I was going to invite you to come to the toilet, if it makes you happy. I am 100 per cent not pregnant; I am 100 per cent not getting married. There are no babies on the agenda.'

She also remained totally unrepentant about the very short timescale between ending things with Pete and starting a new relationship with Alex. 'Have you been through a divorce?' she demanded. 'When you go through a divorce, your life moves on. What am I gonna do, sit at home when the kids go to bed? I am going to go out and socialise. It is not as if I'm an ugly girl and can't pull.'

She continued to hint darkly, too, that Pete was not as single as he was making himself out to be, bringing the name Chantelle into the arena once again. There was no evidence whatsoever that this was true – and both Chantelle and Peter have vigorously denied any romantic involvement – but Katie just couldn't resist it. What's more, it was no longer just about a public bid for sympathy. She had often in the past displayed a talent for mischief-making and it seemed she just couldn't resist making a dig at her ex.

The new series, *What Katie Did Next*, was now making great progress: other than showing the cameras her pregnancy test, Katie displayed a rare moment of sympathy for Pete when shown pictures of him sobbing after the split, then quickly changed tack.

'At the end of the day, he was the one that split with me and I can't get near him – he won't speak to me,' she said. 'I tried to make it work, we had marriage counselling – you name it, it just didn't work. We weren't meant to be. It is finished, over! We have to get divorced and Peter has to find the perfect woman that he wants. He can't control me and I wasn't the one for him, but I'm not that bad, honestly.'

Pete still fumed, however. The picture of Alex's new film continued to upset him and, not for the first time, he made it clear that it was he, and not Alex, who was the children's father. 'As great as Alex may be with the children, he is not their father and never will be,' said a friend. 'As far as Peter is concerned, he is not an ideal father figure and shouldn't be responsible for another man's children – it's not fair on anyone. Pete's number one concern is the welfare of his kids.'

Indeed, there were reports that Pete had been talking to his lawyers to see what he could do about the situation and he was certainly believed to have wanted Katie to split from her new man. 'He has nothing against Alex, but Peter has been rocked by the ongoing revelations about Alex's private life, and now his career,' continued the friend. 'But the crux of the matter is that he and Kate only split up three months ago and she's been dating Alex for a matter of weeks. The kids are having a hard enough time as it is, trying to get to grips with why mummy and daddy no longer live under one roof.'

Pete was, however, moving on too. It was announced that he was to join ITV's *This Morning* in September 2009 as a showbiz reporter and had already done his first gig, interviewing celebrities at the annual MOBO Awards at London's Mayfair Hotel. Network bosses were also said to be lining up another mainstream vehicle for the star.

'Pete will be given all the major A-list celebrity

interviews and sent to all the best gigs,' revealed a source. 'It is a fantastic foot in the door, and ITV have him in mind for a primetime anchoring role.'

Other celebrities who had also signed up to do slots for the show included interior designer Linda Barker, garden designer Diarmuid Gavin and chefs Gino D'Acampo and Jean-Christophe Novelli.

Pete himself was delighted with the new development. 'It should be great,' he said. 'I've loved TV for a long time and I'm in a great position where I can spend time with my kids but I can do TV, music… there's lots of things I can do.'

His professional life might have been going well, but his personal one was still in turmoil, though. Another round of hostilities kicked off when Pete sent Katie a critical text about her behaviour and she did not take it well.

'Katie decided enough was enough, and told Peter in no uncertain terms that she does not want to talk to him ever again,' said a friend. 'She is still hurting after the split, despite trying to put a brave face on things. She feels any contact with Pete really sets her back emotionally and told him so. It is really sad, but she thinks that severing all contact is the way forward.'

Pete retaliated in kind, saying, 'The feeling is mutual.'

A friend revealed, 'Pete's priority is the kids and he appreciates there will undoubtedly be some contact between the two of them because of them, but he feels that it's best for both of them that they speak as little as possible – especially for the time being – as everything is still so raw. You can't blame Peter for texting Katie to express his unhappiness with Alex being pictured with the kids; he is only human and it really hurt. He doesn't blame Katie for her response. In fact, he thinks it is good for both of them.'

For a very short time, the frenzy surrounding the film died down when viewing figures for the reality shows both were filming were announced. To everyone's surprise, Pete won that particular battle, too. On its debut, Katie's show, *What Katie Did Next*, attracted 1.3 million viewers, rising to 1.5 million in the last 15 minutes, while Pete's, *Going It Alone*, pulled in 1.7 million. A source close to Katie insisted she wouldn't have been that concerned – which did not, if one is honest, seem like her normal reaction: Katie is intensely competitive about everything and to see her estranged husband, who she was now treating as the enemy, trouncing her in the ratings would not have amused her.

Indeed, public sentiment came out on a trip to Manchester, where Katie had visited to meet Alex's parents. The couple later went out to the Living Room nightclub, Katie dressed in an outfit reminiscent of the Wild West, when a group of youths began shouting, 'Team Andre!'

Katie actually reacted quite calmly: she merely told them that they should start watching her television show, rather than his. Coincidentally, Pete was also in town, supporting Gay Pride, something that might have influenced the boys.

'Kate was out with pals and determined to let her hair down,' said a friend. 'She'd had a stressful 24 hours meeting her boyfriend's parents for the first time and wanted to unwind, but, when some drunk lads started giving her grief, she found it genuinely upsetting. Kate hates that the public are siding with Peter in the split.'

And they certainly were: Pete had also just been to Brighton's Crazy Bear, where both women and men seemed keen to make his acquaintance: 'At least three women proposed to Pete on stage... even guys were trying to shake his hand afterwards,' said an onlooker. Everywhere he looked, he was winning support.

Pete was also beginning to think about a new relationship, although he wasn't entirely sure if he was ready – and he certainly didn't want to get involved with another fellow celebrity. 'It's a case of once bitten, twice shy,' he said. 'I don't think I would want to be with someone in the industry. If I meet someone, which I'm sure I will, I will try to keep that part of my life private.'

Also, he was trying to hear as little about his ex as he could. 'I've taken off Google alerts, so I don't have to look at it,' Pete continued. 'I just don't want to see it because if I see it, it hurts.'

Speaking at the Edinburgh International TV Festival, Pete also addressed the problem of his children seeing pictures – an increasing number of them – of Alex in his film role and cavorting with their mother. 'I can't control what other people do, only what *I* do,' he conceded frankly. 'Headlines are not the problem. You don't remember the headlines, only pictures of someone acting a certain way.'

And as for, *I'm a Celebrity...* – 'It's something I would love to do again one day,' said Pete.

He was very upset, however, when reports surfaced that Katie was encouraging Harvey to call Alex 'Daddy'. Harvey was not, of course, Pete's biological child, but there had never been any doubt in anyone's mind that Pete was his father figure. To learn that Harvey was being encouraged to look on someone else in that role horrified him.

'Harvey's the one thing Katie's got over Peter,' said

a friend. 'Peter is horrified she's choosing Alex Reid to become a father figure to Harvey; it's devastating to him. Peter may not be Harvey's biological father, but he's been a dad to him since Harvey was one and sees him as a son.

'It breaks Peter's heart when he imagines Princess and Junior visiting him while Harvey has to stay at home, like he has done something wrong.'

It was a difficult situation for everyone, and it was about to get a whole lot worse.

CHAPTER TEN
'I was Raped'

Pete was becoming increasingly agitated about the new man in his children's lives. Worse still were reports that Katie and Alex were thinking about Alex moving in with her, full-time. This distressed Pete even more.

'Peter is very cagey about the move, especially in light of Harvey calling Alex "Daddy",' said the friend. 'He thinks he is losing his kids. He is terrified that Junior and Princess will start following Harvey and call Alex "Dad". Peter thinks that would be the end for him.'

As for Pete himself – 'I think Kate's gone mad,' he said. 'She's not normal at the moment; I thought this would happen.'

His fears were understandable. He wanted to take the children on a short break to Spain and was all set to do just that when, at the very last minute, Katie decided only Junior and Princess should go, and that Harvey should stay at home with her. Pete was distraught.

'He was desperate for a nice family holiday in Spain,' said a friend. 'Everything was organised, but Jordan decided she wanted Harvey to stay with her. It ruined Peter's holiday. He was absolutely gutted and couldn't believe she would do that; it hurt the kids because they were looking forward to their holiday together … It is really upsetting Peter and the kids in equal measures. That's why he wants the divorce settlement to be finalised as soon as possible. He thinks, once he starts seeing the kids regularly, they can be a family again.'

Katie, of course, was equally livid at the idea that she was using the children in her battle with Pete. 'Harvey had appointments at Great Ormond Street Hospital last week – it wasn't a case of Jordan trying to stop him from going away,' said a source close to her. 'Routine is very important to him and she's trying to keep that going for him.

'He [Pete] has been making them [the children] film up to 11pm some days. They're very tired, and she worries about them and wouldn't want to expose Harvey to that. Kate would never stop Pete seeing Harvey. She knows Pete loves Harvey, and Harvey loves Pete. But her main priority is Harvey, as it has to be. And, yes, he is having much more interaction with Alex in the house – but she wants things to develop naturally.'

Katie and Alex, meanwhile, were taking the opportunity to decide where they wanted their relationship to go, and it really did seem to be looking serious. She was beginning to admit privately that she might have been at fault where Pete was concerned and was clearly determined to learn from her mistakes.

'She drove Peter away because she undermined him – and, after a lot of soul-searching, she finally sees what she did to him,' said a source. 'She sat Alex down this week and tearfully told him she will never treat him in such a bad way. Alex is really smitten with her and their chat seemed to clear the air for her, and she wants him to move in. Jordan and Alex have decided they want to be a real couple. She thinks the first step is getting him to move in. He already has a lot of his stuff at hers and at the moment it's a hassle for them to meet up.'

Even as all these negotiations were going on, however, controversy about *Killer Bitch* was still building in the background. Pete himself was disgusted, saying, 'I can't believe he is making films like that. What kind of role model is he for my children?'

But it was Katie's intervention that really set the cat among the pigeons when she revealed that she, too, had been attacked. The reason she spoke out was that Alex was coming under intensive criticism for taking part in something that could appear as somewhat glamorising rape, while Katie was seen to be condoning his stance by standing by her new man.

'Rape is a subject very close to my own heart,' she commented. 'I was raped when I was younger, more than once. Needless to say, I'd never be associated with anything or anyone so sick. I've never talked about this, but I feel I have to because I was so hurt by these accusations that I would not take seriously a subject which affects so many women.

'I urge any woman who has been affected by rape and needs help to talk to somebody they trust about it. I was appalled by the headlines claiming he's taken part in something which glorifies rape. This is completely untrue. He's acting, he didn't have sex – he had his pants on! Someone who was close to Alex was also raped and he is as horrified as I am by these claims.'

Indeed, she felt that any man who committed rape deserved the most severe punishment it was possible to bestow. 'They should get the death penalty,' she stated. 'The way I feel about rapists, they should get an eye for an eye. So, if someone rapes some girl, he should be bent over and the same thing should be done to him.'

Katie had, in fact, had some horrific experiences from very early on, starting when she was just a small child. She'd raised that particular episode in her interview with Piers Morgan. 'Me and two of my friends were sexually assaulted when we were six years old in a local park,' she told him. 'Suddenly a man appeared and promised to buy us an ice cream if we let him touch us. He lined us up, exposed himself and bizarrely began by licking each of us. Then he touched us. I think we all knew it was wrong, but we were paralysed with fear.'

Fortunately, a group of older children saw what was going on and he ran away.

But nothing could have prepared Katie for the reaction to her revelation that she had been raped. In some quarters, astonishment mixed with incredulity surfaced and, not unnaturally, intense speculation began as to who it might have been. All Katie would say was that it was another celebrity, but anyone who thought that someone was about to be outed in a similar way to the Ulrika Jonsson spectacle would be disappointed. Pete knew who it was, according to Katie, but other than that she stayed schtumm.

She was, however, prepared to talk about everything else. Katie made an appearance on *This Morning*, where she tackled a whole range of subjects, beginning with Pete. Yet again she insinuated there was someone else in his life (Chantelle). 'Pete is seeing a girl, it's not come out yet, but it's slowly coming out because I've read about it,' she announced. 'I'll be fine about it though, as long as they are good to the children, that's all I ask.'

Perhaps predictably now, this infuriated Pete. 'He thinks she'll do anything for publicity – even spouting blatant lies like these,' said a friend.

Again, Pete threatened to sue over the allegations. Nor was he thrilled about what Katie came up with next.

'I think Pete has got more hatred for me than anything, because of Alex or whatever,' said Katie. 'He does hate me – he just so obviously does. He calls me vile, he calls me everything, and that's fine. If I'm honest, I think it backfired on him. I think he probably thought we would get back together, but the media got involved and it got worse and worse.'

She then turned her attention to her new man. The furore over the film was still going strong, the recent revelations from his ex-girlfriends were still fresh in the memory and who knew what might come out next? But apparently it didn't worry Katie in the slightest.

'I love it that Alex has had a past,' she declared. 'There's more surprises to come out about him and I can't wait. He is a lovable guy.' (She was certainly right about the surprises, too.)

Then there was the Brazilian banker Andre Pinto, who had given a lurid account of the fling they had together. It seemed nothing could faze Katie. 'That Brazilian!' she cried. 'I've never had a kiss and tell, and no one's ever done that on me, what an idiot. Three times I was with him and it wasn't even third-time lucky – it was rubbish!'

That was Pinto taken care of. She then got on to the subject of her partying lifestyle, which was still causing a lot of po-faces, especially when it came to her mothering skills.

'Of course [I feel like I'm being painted as the Devil] but at the end of the day, I am living my life the way it is, I'm not going to change just because people are saying, "You should calm down." So what? I do what I want to do,' she declared. 'I'm not even doing anything bad, but they [the media] don't want to write that I went to the New Forest in my pink horsebox, cooking a roast dinner, doing normal things or the good things that happen... it's all the bad things.'

There was, in fact, something admirable about this attitude: Katie was living life entirely on her own terms and not doing what other people thought she should be doing simply to look good. She was an independent spirit, feisty with it and wasn't letting herself be messed about by anyone. And that was, perhaps, behind the next line of questioning, namely why she didn't come across as upset.

'I can't help it that I'm so strong! I've got hurt in the past and I know how to switch off,' Katie replied. 'Anyone out there who has a break-up – if the guy isn't interested, don't sit around and mope about it, get on with your life! That's just the way I am, I can't help that.'

And finally, as for Alex himself – 'Do I love him?' Katie ruminated. 'That's quite a strong word! I might've kissed him on the lips, and I'm very much involved with him. He's a loveable guy and he's so down-to-earth and very good with the kids, and I love having him around.'

That reference to kissing on the lips was a curious one – matters were widely believed to have gone a lot further than that – but, in all other respects, the message was clear: Katie was back in charge of her life, she was over Pete and had moved on.

But, while Katie might have been doing as she liked, the initial stage of the divorce was now only days away, and there was real concern that she might end up with custody or financial issues. Pete had already said he didn't want a penny from her, but that didn't mean she might not have to pay up should he change his mind. And then, of course, there were the children. Pete had not exactly been reticent when it came to voicing concerns about the three of them spending time with Alex; nor had Katie been doing herself much good.

'Price's behaviour over the last four months is probably going to contribute to the custody arrangements, especially her well-publicised trips to Ibiza,' commented Ambi Sitham, a distinguished showbiz lawyer. 'She was obviously getting very drunk. In addition, she has exposed her children at a very young age to a new relationship with Alex Reid. They will look into his background and at his suitability as a potential stepfather to Price's children. The courts will not look favourably on anyone they deem a bad role model.

'I should think the least the judge would decide is to grant joint custody of the children to Price and Andre. He might even get sole custody. Andre, coming from a strong Greek-Cypriot family background, has conducted himself as the model father.'

As for the division of the spoils – Katie was estimated to have earned about £20 million since the wedding and Pete might possibly have a claim for about a quarter of that. 'The courts will look at what role was played in emotional support, as well as financial,' said Ambi. 'Andre will be able to show he contributed to the Katie Price brand. Before they met, she was purely known as Jordan the glamour model. As a result of marrying Andre, she was able to create an alter ego. I think she is in line for a bit of a shock. She will not be walking away from this without making a substantial payout.'

On 9 September 2009, a judge in the High Court's Family Division in London granted a decree nisi, with a six-week cooling-off period before the decree absolute. Proceedings took less than a minute and neither Katie nor Pete was present – Katie was at home with her horses, while Pete was on his *This Morning* slot.

Now, it really was all over bar the shouting (in reality, there was still a fair bit of shouting to come), but the issue of rape that Katie had raised so graphically shortly beforehand continued to linger. It was a subject that simply would not go away.

CHAPTER ELEVEN

Fighting Back

Katie attempted to shrug off both the end of her marriage and the ongoing row over the rape allegations. She and Alex declared their intention to fight each other in the ring: they were to take part in a girls versus boys 'extreme combat' session, though this was purely for show. Katie was to team up with Michelle Heaton, while Alex's fighting partner would be Hugh Hanley.

'It's going to be a real crowd pleaser,' said Sol Gilbert, Katie's trainer and the person who brought her together with Alex. 'I'm sure there'll be plenty of interest. She's got all the moves, too. Alex will have to watch out! I've taken a few punches from her and she's as tough as they come.

'I've been training Jordan and she can deliver some really special right hooks. She's shown a real flair for it and is getting better every day. But, at the end of the day, this is just a showcase boys against girls bout. It will be fun and not at all dangerous, like the real thing.'

When the duo actually attended an Extreme Brawl Fighting Championship event, however, matters turned rather nasty. Two fighters had been drinking all evening, and one punched Alex, while Katie was pushed to the floor. 'One of the fighters fancied his chances and wanted to prove himself by asking Alex to step outside,' explained the promoter, Andy Jardine. 'Alex said, "I'm not being funny, but you've just had your first fight and lost, and I've fought some of the best in the world." He didn't like that answer and the fight started there.'

Others insisted there was a little more to it than that. 'He wound me up,' said one of the other fighters present. 'He's an arrogant wanker, who was walking around like he owned the place! We had a problem with him and were going to sort it out, but he chickened out. He deserves to get his head kicked in.'

In the meantime, Katie was very ostentatiously showing Pete that she didn't care any more. 'It's been a nightmare, but we're finally getting there,' she told a friend. 'I just want to move on with my life and

Peter proves he's still got what it takes as he performs on a Manchester street as part of a prize for a local radio station listener. *Inset*: Taking time to speak to his fans.

Victory! A delighted Pete greets the Press outside the Royal Courts of Justice after he accepted substantial damages over untrue newspaper claims that he had been unfaithful to his wife.

Getting on with his life and career as a single man.

Above: At the Silver Clef awards with Denise Van Outen.

Below left: No guessing who Pete's just been talking to.

Below right: Were they, weren't they? They weren't.

Above left: Pete shows off his new physique.

Above right: Out and about with friends.

Below: Pete's family are a vital part of his support network and have helped him get through difficult times. He is pictured here with his mother, brother and sister in Brighton.

Above and below left: Pete is often quoted as saying that his kids are his life now. Here he is spending time with Junior and Princess.

Below right: Comforting a distressed Junior as he hands him over to the nanny.

At the launch of his album, *Revelation*.

Pete Power – 6000 fans turn up to an album signing and, *below right*, make it clear who they are rooting for.

Pete in his element on the stage.

think about the future – one without Pete. It's sad, but I have to face facts. Thank God it's over!'

Pete, however, confined himself to the screens of *This Morning*.

'Are you aware that you're getting divorced today?' asked Eamonn Holmes.

'Really?' said Pete. 'Well, yeah, just before I came in, I was told that it's been accepted.'

'So you don't have to go to court?' asked Ruth Langsford.

'Well, if I do I'm in trouble because I'm here on the sofa,' Pete replied.

Almost immediately, however, it was reported that Katie's act of bravado for the public was very different to what she really wanted. Just two weeks before the divorce went through, she was said to have sent Pete a series of texts, asking him to give them another chance. 'Pete, you were my fairytale,' said one, followed by 'I still love you – give us another chance. X' and 'Why can't it go back to how it used to be – you, me, J, P and H?'

But it was far, far too late for that now. Too much had been said and done, and there was no going back on a relationship that was well and truly over.

'Pete was angered and hurt by the stories Katie was spreading about him in various TV and magazine interviews,' said a source. 'She claimed that he had a girlfriend, which is utter rubbish, and implied that he was not over her. Again, this is total nonsense. Kate must still have feelings by behaving the way she's been acting. From the timing of the text, it seemed as if Katie was alone and had possibly had a couple of drinks. There is no way she would be sending those kind of messages with Alex in the room with her and I doubt that he'll be pleased.

'Pete has remained 100 per cent faithful and celibate since the split and is completely over Kate. He would never go back. And contrary to reports, he does not hate her. Pete simply wants the pair to get on and be civil for the sake of their children.'

Katie denied sending the texts, saying that she had lost her phone and perhaps a friend had done it for a laugh. Pete did not deny receiving the texts, saying, with some justification, 'They've left me a bit speechless, to be honest. She's introduced this Alex guy to our kids, but, if he is so important to her, then why is she still texting me, telling me she loves me?' Why, indeed?

Behind the scenes, in fact, Katie was feeling pretty miserable. 'I'm like a swan,' she told a friend. 'Serene and calm on top but, underneath the water, I'm paddling like hell!'

She also decided not to have a divorce party and some reports had it that she was tiring of Alex now that the divorce had finally come through.

'Katie never really thought the divorce would happen – half of her wishes she could turn the clock back,' said a friend. 'Pete let himself grieve after the split whereas Katie just hit the party scene hard to show him she didn't care – now the reality is coming crashing in on her that it really is over for ever. She is niggly with people and down – she sometimes just wants to sit in front of the TV with a pack of chocolate HobNobs. But she always wants someone with her – she can't bear to be alone. It's as if she's scared of stopping and thinking about what's happening.'

And there continued to be concerns about what was happening to her image. Quite apart from the wildness and the partying, there were now the rape allegations and the cage fighting, hardly the sort of things that the mothers of the girls who were Katie's fans would want their daughters to know about.

'Sales of the horse books and clothes are dependent largely on mums buying them for their daughters and so image is important,' commented a source. 'She is constantly on the web, reading all the internet hate mail posted about her. She is genuinely worried about public opinion. She's been saying, "People don't like me any more."

'The equestrian stuff really needs her to be perceived as respectable Katie Price, the horseriding mother of three, not Jordan who rampages drunk round nightclubs, pulling men. She frets that she's damaged her image, quite possibly beyond repair, and they haven't settled the financial split of their marriage. At the moment, Peter is set to get half of all the marital assets – which is a lot of money for her to kiss goodbye to. Peter is an annoyance in her head and she's seething that he is, in her mind, cashing in on his emotions all the time with sympathetic magazine deals and flogging his album, which is out on Monday.'

As if all that were not enough, there was trouble in paradise: reports stated that Katie was beginning to tire of her new man. That was hardly surprising, given that she was clearly still so cut up over Pete, but it wasn't helping her state of mind. And so she started thinking that Alex should do what Katie herself had done so often – have surgery.

'Katie has apparently said he should look into having plastic surgery,' a source revealed. 'She suggested he should have his ears pinned back, some Botox and his nose straightened. It was a half-joke, but she is getting a bit weary of him. Alex thinks that, despite everything she says, she is still in love with Peter and Alex has told her to make up her mind about what she wants. Kate thinks having a man on her arm makes her feel needed, sexy and successful, but her close pals know she's looking sad, lonely and almost a bit desperate even.'

Hardly the image she wanted to project. Nor, despite the fact that they were officially divorced, was the war between Kate and Pete calming down. Pete's new album was out and he launched it at London's Studio Valbonne on 14 September: a team of celebrities were to hand, including another erstwhile *I'm A Celebrity...* contestant, Nicola McLean. She was happily married to the Peterborough United player Tommy Williams, but was content to blow kisses at a huge poster of Pete, while confessing that she 'fancied Peter massively' when she was at school. 'I loved him,' she said. 'I used to write "Nicola McLean 4 Peter Andre" on my school notebook. Katie will hate me for saying that, but then she hates everybody!'

The evening turned out to be a highly emotional one for Pete. Dedicating the song 'Unconditional' to Harvey, he sang his heart out and was so moved that he wept as soon as he was backstage once more. 'When Pete came backstage, it all went a bit quiet and he started to cry,' commented an observer. 'He really broke down because Harvey means so much to him.'

The next day it was the turn of the fans. Indeed, such was the public appetite that over a thousand fans, mainly teenage girls, turned out to see Pete when he launched the album at HMV in Birmingham's Bullring. Many had waited for hours just to see him.

Katie chose this moment to hint, yet again, at the presence of another woman in his life. 'He dropped the kids off with a girl in his car on Sunday,' she explained. 'They kissed on the lips, so it must be his girlfriend.'

But the usual denials promptly came forth from Team Pete.

Katie really caused a rumpus, however, when she spoke on television's *The Wright Stuff on Five* – hosted, coincidentally enough, by Matthew Wright, the man who, mistakenly and in fact wrongly, outed John Leslie as the alleged attacker of Ulrika Jonsson. Like Katie, Ulrika had never named her attacker. Katie was asked to explain what had encouraged her to open up as she did.

'I haven't just come out and said I was raped,' said Katie. 'I was sticking up for Alex. I basically said I would never go out with a rapist. I've been raped, someone close to Alex has been raped, so that's how it's got all out of context. I think it is so out of order when people say I am trying to do it for sympathy; that is so wrong.

'I'm absolutely livid – I mentioned it in my column and then I done a shoot with the kids last week and they just tried to press on and on about it, and I said, "I'm not going to say who it is." And they just dig and dig and dig. It has been blown out of all context – I've woken up this morning and it's on the covers of all the newspapers, and I'm like, "Oh, my God!"'

Was she, asked Wright, planning to notify the police? 'It happened absolutely years ago and, like anyone, it's just a hard thing to do,' said Katie. 'It's been there and done now, so what do you do? If something happens, you should go to the police. Maybe I should have done. I went back and said to my friends, "This happened ..."'

'It was definitely rape – I didn't consent to it. What do you do? It's a difficult situation: I just don't want to bring it all up and it has been brought up. I'm not here to say who it is. Really, I haven't slept with that many people, let's be honest – it's just the papers make out I have, and I haven't. And this happened years ago, way before Pete, and I don't have to lie about it. I'm shocked this has come out just because I was sticking up for Alex.'

But that was not the end to the affair. Katie had also been quoted as saying, 'A famous celebrity raped me and Peter knows who it was. It was years ago before I was with Pete, and my friends and family knew about it at the time.'

Pete, however, point-blank denied that he'd known about any such thing, leading Katie to add that she had 'no idea' why he denied it. 'He's not the Pete I knew any more,' she said sadly. 'He's being really cruel, when he knows exactly who did it.'

The battle between the two went on. Katie had just been on daytime TV, so now Pete did the same, ostensibly to publicise his new album, but also to put a few pertinent points to rest. He appeared on *This Morning* to sing 'Call The Doctor' and answer more questions about his personal life.

Host Phillip Schofield kicked off by asking him about the texts that Katie was reputed to have sent.

'OK, I'm going to tell the truth here. I was getting texts. I knew that was going to come out,' said Pete. 'I knew someone was going to say something about that. And you know what? What would I need to lie about something like that? I don't want to come on here and say something bad about her, or bad about anything, it's just that that was something that happened.'

And then there were Katie's constant claims that, contrary to appearances, Pete had a new girlfriend. Now he looked exasperated. 'First of all, there will come a point where I'm going to meet someone, and it hasn't happened yet,' he said, 'but it's a very clever thing that she's done because it means, whoever I end up with in the future, she's going to say, "Ah, see I told you!" and, in that way, you might think you can't win, but it's just a silly little game. There's no point in going tit for tat.'

And so the battle went on. Neither would calm down, and Katie, in her hurt, just continued to lash out – but to no avail.

CHAPTER TWELVE

Who Was It?

Pete's denial that he knew anything about the attack certainly hadn't calmed matters down. By this time speculation was rife as to the man's identity, although Katie was still refusing point-blank to name him, with intense and lurid speculation surfacing all over the internet. However, more details about the attack were coming into the open, although not from Katie herself, including a very nasty description about her throat being grabbed. 'She told how he became violent towards her after not getting his way,' revealed a friend. 'At one point he made a move for her throat – it sounded terrible. It was like she had been hardened up by what had happened. At the time, she was too scared to report it.'

KATIE V PETER – THE DIVORCE

It happened after the two of them had been on a series of 'secret dates' and had seemed to be getting on well. However, there had been early warnings that all might not be well. 'She was shocked by some of the lewd things he used to come out with,' continued the friend. 'It was clear he was highly sexed and, in hindsight, it should have served as a warning sign. She wishes she had nothing to do with him.'

Keen to turn people's attention to other aspects of her life, Katie gave an extensive interview, in which she tackled some of the more controversial moments in her recent past. This started with the wild behaviour and then, of course, her new relationship with Alex.

'When I split from Pete, everyone said I had to lie low and stay in,' she said. 'But I was the one who'd been dumped. Am I supposed to sit here and wait for him to say: "Right, Kate, you can have a boyfriend now, you can do this, you can do that"? If he doesn't want me, I'm going to live my life. Pete is always being pictured with the kids and I don't want to play that game. It's like Monopoly – and I'm in jail. I've run out of "Get out of jail free" cards. But it's all fun and games... whatever dice is thrown next, bring it on!' It was typical Katie: always bouncing back and fighting on.

Surely, though, she was asked, the bad publicity could be disheartening? 'I've been doing this job since I was 17, I've been in relationships and split up,' declared Katie. 'I've always come out worst; it's nothing new. The split was a big shock, but I accepted it and dealt with it; I moved on. My mum was the same when she split up with my dad – she moved straight on. It was Pete who wanted to end it. I would never, ever have ended our marriage. Never, ever! I would have always given it a go. We tried counselling, but it didn't work. I suppose it's a relief that I'm out of it now and I'm not going back.'

It didn't appear that she had the option, but Katie did hint at another possible cause of the break-up – her drinking or, more specifically, Pete's attitude towards it. 'Pete is the only guy who has ever been annoyed with me drinking,' she said. 'When I was with Pete, I didn't go out because it would cause an argument and I couldn't be bothered to argue. In the past he was my perfect partner, my prince. But we didn't get on – the fairy tale ended. He was a lovely guy when I was with him. I don't know the Pete he is now. When I met him, he owned a gym in Cyprus. Did he forget where he came from?'

That, of course, harked back to the competition between them, which was clearly as strong as ever.

Pete's music career appeared to be resurging: the album had elicited a huge amount of interest and he was doing well. The televised row they had had about which of them was the better known was looking more than a little ironic now.

But Katie, as ever, was adopting a pragmatic approach to her life. She hadn't denied that she'd suffered. but people, she maintained, grew that way. 'People need to be heartbroken,' she said. 'People need to hurt to know how to make themselves strong. I've been hurt in the past; that's probably why I dealt with the Pete thing so well. I never trust a man 100 per cent – I don't think anyone should.'

She was also showing a distinctly mischievous streak. Pete had just been on nationwide television talking about the texts that she had sent, begging him to go back. Katie retaliated by hinting that the truth was: he wasn't over her.

'What I reckon is that it's all backfired on him, which is why he doesn't want to see me – because he's still got feelings,' said Katie happily. 'I'm the one who's been dumped, yet I'm quite happy to sit in a room with him and talk about the kids, no hard feelings. But he doesn't seem to want to sit in a room with me.'

Of course, there were explanations for that other

than Pete having feelings for Katie, but it was a point well made.

In actual fact, Pete appeared to be softening his stance. There was never going to be the chance of a romantic reconciliation, but he was prepared to concede that, in the future, they might be able to get on a little better with one another than they had been doing.

'I have said before that I reckon, for the sake of the kids, you will compromise and do things, and I think, yes, there will be a point,' he conceded. 'So you know you've got to allow time for things to settle, I think. I have thought about it for the kids, but not how, or when or whatever. I just know that time is a healer, everybody says that.' And so it was proving for both.

But the growing row over the rape claim refused to go away. By now, Katie was being urged by all sections of the media to name her attacker and she appeared to do so, completely inadvertently, while filming *What Katie Did Next*. She was off camera, but the allegation, which could have had severe legal ramifications, was heard by a number of people standing around: they were all informed that they must not, under any circumstances, put the name into the public arena. 'A handful of people know who was allegedly named, but they are absolutely not allowed to even tell their loved ones,' said a source. And so they complied.

'Surrey Police treats all reports of sexual offences very seriously and investigates them thoroughly, encouraging anyone who may have been a victim to come forward and providing specialist officers to support them,' said a spokesman. 'Based on our enquiries and the lack of substantiated information – particularly around locations and dates of any allegations – we have recorded an incident, but due to its very historic nature we are dependent on Miss Price's co-operation to formally record a crime and continue any investigation. Should any new information come to light, it will be diligently investigated and this position may be reviewed.'

Katie herself was said to be 'hugely relieved', telling friends, 'I never expected it to blow up like this – I want it to go away.'

In the wake of the claims, she was pictured arriving at Biggin Hill airbase in her pink Beetle, and taking off to the skies shortly afterwards in a helicopter to an unnamed destination.

Still more details about the attack continued to emerge. Katie had got into bed with him, but made it obvious that she didn't want to have sex. 'I said no –

but he wouldn't take no for an answer,' she told a friend. To make matters worse, the two of them had bumped into one another at a celebrity gathering, a couple of months on. 'He said, "How about a blowjob?"' Katie related. 'I was horrified and burst into tears. Now, every time I see his face on TV, I shudder. It brings back such horrible memories.'

As for those who still doubted her version of events, the friend was certain she was genuine. 'It was obvious to me that she was completely sincere about it all – she didn't want to go to the police because she didn't want to have to go through it all with strangers.'

And so, the furore hadn't gone away, nor had the war between Pete and Kate. Pete continued to be mobbed, next by a 9,000-strong crowd, who queued for five hours to see him in a record shop in Havant. Twelve women fainted and ambulances were called.

Meanwhile, Katie found herself in a very different mêlée. She and Alex attended a cage fight in Limehouse, East London, in which Alex was fighting. When his name was read out over the tannoy, there were boos from the 2,000-strong crowd. Katie made some very offensive gestures, yelling, 'Fuck you! Fuck you!'

But the crowd was most emphatically not with

him. Throughout, they shouted for his opponent; 'Mason, Mason, Mason!' Nor was Alex thrilled to discover that his opponent had landed the VIP dressing room, while he had to make do with something much smaller.

'Clearly, people were trying to tell them something,' said a source.

Combat commenced, as Alex took on City banker Jack Mason. After three rounds, Alex won the Thai boxing middleweight title match. As the audience looked on, Katie promptly stripped down to her underwear, replaced the dress she had been wearing with a mini-number emblazoned with sequins that read 'The Champ', and climbed into the ring to tell her man that she was proud.

The crowd begged to differ: Alex had won on points and not everyone agreed with the outcome, erupting into boos again. 'It was amazing,' said an onlooker. 'She stood there in the centre of the cage, flicking V-signs at the crowd, shouting, "Come on then, if you think you're hard enough!" The crowd just erupted because they all thought Alex had lost the bout and Jordan was just being so provocative.'

Another observer had a different take on it, noting that Katie had been very pleasant on arrival, but perhaps it wasn't the best idea to stand up so vociferously for her man – in those surroundings, at least. 'She was as sweet as they come,' he said. 'She was clearly very upset by the way the fans treated Alex, but I don't think she did him any favours. He's not much of a fighter, if he needs his girlfriend to stick up for him.'

They went off to celebrate with some champagne, while Katie ostentatiously showed off a ring on her engagement finger, forcing her friend Michelle Heaton to deny the couple had wedding plans.

Underneath all the bravado, however, it was a different matter. In private, Katie was said to have told Alex, 'Everyone's against me, everyone's against us – we must be the most hated couple in Britain!' And she continued to talk about the split with Pete. It was his jealousy of Andrew Gould, she said now, that had been at the root of the problem. Then there had been the night out, in which she was photographed drinking with other men, one of whom would turn out to be Andrew.

'I said Pete would go mad if he knew I was out with Andrew because he had a problem with him, but everyone was saying, "Don't be silly, you're a grown woman! He's here with [his wife] Polly,"' she related. 'Pete didn't ask who was there, so I didn't mention Andrew. I was pictured on the front page with a "mystery man", but the guy was gay and someone Pete had met before. But straight away I felt sick: I wanted to get out of the house and avoid a confrontation with Pete because I knew he'd be angry. On the way to Andrew's stables, I was hyperventilating.'

Andrew and Polly certainly backed up her claims. Katie related how Pete had got very upset and started quizzing her about a McDonald's receipt in her handbag. Andrew confirmed he had heard a conversation on Katie's mobile. 'She put him on loudspeaker and he said, "If I see him, I will knock him out." I suddenly thought, God, he really doesn't like me. He was yelling, "So, you were driving along, having a McDonald's, playing the happily married couple together."'

Polly had the same sense that Pete had a colder side. 'The first time we met him, he was asking us all these questions about our relationship, including questioning Andrew about what he thought about false breasts. It felt like we were being quizzed. We only met him a handful of times, though, because he wasn't interested in Kate's riding.'

It was a different picture of Pete from the one usually played out: clearly, there had been jealous tantrums, rages and rows about Katie's drinking.

Still, they had been married and Katie had not wanted their relationship to end. Though she was putting an enormously brave face on it, her ongoing obsession made it clear that she still had feelings for Pete, ones that just refused to go away.

At least the rape allegations, something Katie clearly regretted had ever seen the light of day, were being talked about less. But events were about to gather momentum: for a start, one person who had been conspicuous in his silence over the relationship between Pete and Harvey had been Harvey's biological father, Dwight Yorke. Now he was preparing to speak out – and very uncomfortable reading it made, too.

But an even bigger story was about to break. For some time now, it had been understood that Katie's new lover was not afraid to push boundaries, as was about to become abundantly clear. The nation could hardly believe what they were about to hear – a cage fighter wearing a dress?

CHAPTER THIRTEEN
Katie's Men

In a life so publicly led, there was one oddity in the story of Katie and Pete: the silence of Dwight Yorke. Not only had he never commented publicly on his 18 months with Katie, he also remained silent on the subject of Pete's relationship with Harvey, something that had become particularly complicated since the divorce. But now, at last, he was speaking out. Dwight had written his autobiography, *Born to Score* (released at the end of September 2009 and published by Macmillan), and, for the first time, his take on the relationship and all its ramifications came out.

For a start, to no one's surprise, he had been extremely concerned when Katie found out that she was pregnant. 'My reaction was immediate,' he said. 'There was no way we could have this baby. I told her, "Our relationship is too unstable. I don't think it's right."'

Of course, Katie went ahead and had Harvey, but did not appear to tone down her partying one jot, much to Dwight's concern. 'I challenged her about this lifestyle,' he continued. 'She'd desperately wanted our baby, but was this her idea of motherhood? I'm not by nature a bitter person, but no one's driven me quite so close to that as Katie. The woman is infuriating!'

A brief reconciliation followed, with a holiday in Barbados and Tobago, during the course of which Yorke gave Katie an expensive ring.

When the couple visited Dwight's mother in Tobago, Katie didn't want to let her look after Harvey, which deeply concerned Dwight and proved to be the final straw for him. Dwight decided the relationship could not go any further and it came to an end.

Of course, Harvey went on to acquire a new father figure in the form of Pete, but Dwight was none too impressed by him, either. 'When I met Andre, I wanted to throttle him,' he said. 'I'm not a violent man and it takes an awful lot to rile me, but this man got under my skin at the outset.'

Dwight went on to say that Katie and Peter's house was filled with photographs of the two of them. 'I couldn't walk down a hallway without his preening mug staring back at me or the pair of them draped over each other. No way would I ever, ever allow Harvey to be adopted by him!'

Pete, unsurprisingly, was deeply wounded by the remarks. 'I do not hate Dwight and didn't realise he felt that way about me,' he said carefully, before adding, 'But I have been a real father to Harvey and he calls me "Daddy" — I guess that sticks in Dwight's throat.'

Katie herself was livid, and was considering legal action. 'Katie loves Harvey to pieces and has always encouraged Dwight to stay in touch with Harvey,' said a source. 'She wants her little boy to know his father and know where he came from. Dwight has made out he's a diligent dad, but Katie claims he last saw Harvey last October, almost a year ago to the day. Harvey has a full-time nanny and, as part of the terms of employment, she is allowed to take Harvey up to visit Dwight, whenever he wants. She says Dwight has not made an attempt in the past 12 months to use this clause.

'Katie has never, ever complained about Harvey's disabilities, or the care and attention he requires on a daily basis. She does everything for him to make his quality of life as good as possible. Kate has been advised to see her lawyers, to see if she wants to look at the maintenance agreement again. She is not best pleased by the accusations in his book.'

It was hard not to understand the point she was making. While Dwight maintained contact with his child, it was Katie – and Pete – who brought the boy up and, naturally, they were angered by the criticisms. But they could no longer be united in the face of anyone else's ideas – they were fighting their battles separately now.

Once Dwight reappeared, he became part of the drama, too. He infuriated Katie by suggesting that Harvey was not so ill as she made out. 'I don't think they are as bad as she's making them out to be,' he said. 'He's got perfect hands, perfect feet – he runs around, he comes in the house, he turns on his DVD... He does all those things.'

But Katie, pointing out that Dwight had seen Harvey only once in the previous year, was having none of it. 'Dwight has never shown any interest in finding out more about Harvey and his disabilities,' she snapped. 'If he had ever attended any hospital appointments, he would understand Harvey's condition.'

Meanwhile, Dwight had no qualms about pointing out the difference between Katie and Jordan, even when they were in bed. According to Dwight, making love to Katie was a caring and warm experience, whereas when he had sex with the Jordan side of the personality, antics in the bedroom became much more wild and voracious.

Something that Alex was no doubt still finding out. However, rumours persisted that Katie was still obsessed with Pete. As well as those texts, another story emerged that, just before the divorce, she had left a message on his answering machine, which was, in fact, a rendition of 'I Will Always Love You'.

In the light of this, it was less than surprising when reports surfaced that Katie was not happy with the new nanny, Nita, that Pete had taken on: on the grounds that she was too pretty. This, in turn, was said to have provoked another row with Alex. She already knew Nita – she and Pete had interviewed her for the role a couple of years earlier – but it was only now, post-divorce, that Pete got in touch to see if she was free.

'The poor girl!' Pete protested. 'She only started with us a week ago. She is a really lovely person, just really genuine and kind. I did warn her it's a bit of a mad world. The kids have really bonded with her.

Princess is really, really close to her. It's great that she has that girlie influence in my home now.'

To say any woman was bonding with the children would be bound to aggravate Katie, but Pete might be forgiven for relishing the moment: after all, he had had to put up with watching Alex larking about with them for weeks now.

And so the war raged on. Katie was a guest at Simon Cowell's high-profile birthday party in early October 2009. Given her comments about him earlier that summer, there was some speculation that she thought her future might lie with him. 'Jordan sees Simon as her dream man,' said a source. 'He is the most powerful man in the entertainment industry and his party was billed as the biggest showbiz event of the year. Jordan sees him as the perfect catch – powerful and sexy, a bloke who she can rely on and trust.

'She knows that Simon is so respected that he could never make a fool out of her. Both her husband Peter Andre and her boyfriend Alex have done things which have caused her embarrassment and made her look a fool. She knows, if she was with Simon, her career would be back on track instantly. She would have the credibility she has lost in recent months. She doesn't just want him for that reason, though: the more she has got to know Simon, the sexier she thinks he is.'

It seemed Simon was a fan of Katie's, too. 'She's fun,' he once said. 'I like her. Give the girl a chance, we all make mistakes.'

And, in the event, Katie attended with Alex in tow – turning up very late and very drunk indeed. She was seen staggering to the top table to talk to Simon before being led away again, seemingly the worse for wear.

Hostilities did not calm down: rather, they heated up quite considerably when Pete's album, *Revelations*, was screened during the advertisement breaks on *What Katie Did Next*. The lady herself went ballistic. 'She was really cross about it and accused Pete of using her popularity to sell his records,' said a source. 'Katie and her team thought it was a real low blow and tried to see if they could put a stop to it. But Pete's management had bought the advertising time, fair and square. Katie has a real problem with people using her to further themselves and she thought that was what Pete was doing. She definitely didn't see the funny side – she thought he was taking advantage of her.'

At this point, war broke out on another front. It sometimes seemed that, just as one feud went quiet, another hotted up, and so it was, when Dwight slouched back into the shadows, Alex's ex-girlfriend

Marie Thornett stepped up to the pitch. And, in fairness to Katie, Marie started it: she posted a private message on Alex's Facebook entry that was almost bound to have Katie bouncing off the walls, not least because it referred to some photos of Pete that were still up in the house.

'Hi Reidy,' it began. 'Hope you are doing ok. Just wondering if you needed a photo of me to put by your bed, because I have read that Katie sleeps with one of peter next to her. I can send you one if need be, but im sure you have plenty :). Hope this made you smile XXX.'

And, if it did, it certainly didn't go well with Katie. Still smarting over the ads fiasco, she certainly didn't hold back and started posting messages herself: 'Marie stop being such a desperate slag you had your chance with Alex so stop sending him begging emails you were shit in bed an couldn't except him so jog on ps thanks for being a great fan an fuck off.'

Strong stuff, but not enough to calm Katie down – minutes later, a second post appeared: 'Oh forgot lets see if Marie the slag sells this to the papers cheap fucking loser no wonder Alex didn't want you dnt forget to put in the artical you didn't have sex for 8 months boring slut.'

Marie, who had not been on the receiving end of

one of Katie's missiles before, was stunned. 'When I saw what she wrote, I was numb with shock,' she said. 'I rang my mum, who told my sister, and she was so infuriated she put a posting on the wall, giving her a piece of her mind.'

Indeed, she did. Marie's sister Hannah, 16, who is studying for her A-levels, leaped into action and started posting herself. 'Shut up you sad woman,' she wrote, 'you need to grow up to be honest your a mess sort yourself out my love. Wipedy doo your famous and tbh [to be honest] i'm a 16 year old and i think your an extreme alcoholic mess. pretty sad really. My sister is beautiful, classy and has everything you haven't really. Wow your famous but have a think before you think your better than everyone else because trust me you're not.'

In true Katie style, she refused to take this lying down. Moments later, another post appeared. 'Famous yeah, something you an your sister will never be only for selling stories on real genuine people. Maybe you should read Marie's messages before commenting. Thanks for being fans I love you for it :) lol.'

It was all getting a little out of hand: in truth, Katie was acting unwisely in allowing herself to be drawn into rows with people who were little more than children. At this point, Marie decided to calm matters down. 'In the end, I had enough,' she said. 'I decided to send a private message to Alex's Facebook email.' However, this message, too, found its way into the public domain. 'What wonderful words of wisdom and a great use of vocabulary,' it read. 'You might want to use spell-check and look up the meaning of slut. I have the emails still and I would not say they are begging. I think you need to check certain facts as well. I'm happy for Alex, that you accept him for who he really is. Didn't realise this would cause you to have such an outrageous outburst. Are you feeling a little insecure? XX.'

There was no reply. Shortly afterwards, Marie and Hannah unsurprisingly disappeared from the list of Alex's friends. Hannah herself had been horrified by the experience. 'When I read what Katie Price said, I thought it was disgusting that a grown woman and someone so famous had said that. The language she used was horrible. I used to be a real fan and I'd watch her and Peter's programme, but I'm not now. I'm on Team Andre now. But what is also cruel is the fact she took the Mickey we were her fans. She should never forget fans made her.'

Marie had not been impressed by the whole episode, either. 'It's ironic,' she said. 'When I

Katie's book launches are always a spectacle. The event for her style book, *Standing Out*, was no exception as she played up to press stories about boyfriend Alex Reid being a cross-dresser.

Above left: Alex as alter-ego Roxanne – dressed in Katie's revealing Ibiza outfit.

Above right: Katie signs books for the fans.

Below: It wasn't just Alex who took part in the launch. Pictured next to him is Katie's riding instructor Andrew Gould in her equestrian clothing; brother Danny in Katie's wedding outfit and friend Phil Turner in her Jordan racing team colours.

Above left: Happy families? Katie and Alex attend a premiere together with Katie's kids and Alex's nephew.

Above right: The couple after Alex won a cage-fighting bout. Katie changed into this dress to celebrate his victory.

Below left: Alex watches as Katie promotes her equestrian gear.

Below right: Katie gets upset with the paparazzi. © *Getty Images*

Alex spends some time getting to know Katie and her kids on a family day out. Reportedly, Pete was less than happy when Alex was pictured with his children.

Head to head in the ITV2 ratings war. Both couples promote their respective fly-on-the-wall shows for the channel and, *below*, Katie with her camera crew.

Above: Mother love – quality time with Princess and Junior.

Below: Katie's pink customised horsebox and mobile home.

Pete has always cited Michael Jackson as a big influence on him. Here, he is pictured with brother Mike at the premiere of the Jackson film, *This is It*.

Who knows what the future holds for the media's favourite subjects …

watched their TV show last Thursday, I didn't think she was that bad. But I have now had first-hand experience of her spiteful side. I was horrified at her vile language – it was disgusting. I have never felt any maliciousness towards Katie, but she is clearly threatened by the fact Alex loved me.'

A friend of Katie's was lofty. 'This girl has been constantly hounding Alex, asking him to get back with her, which obviously angers Katie because it's disrespectful,' she said. 'They know full well he is in a relationship.'

Indeed, he was – and what revelations were about to come out of that relationship.

CHAPTER FOURTEEN

A Lady Called Roxanne

What happened next, however, astonished even seasoned Katie watchers, for she was about to shock her public to its very core. She had, as mentioned, been very drunk at Simon Cowell's party, and had shown some pictures of Alex on her phone to fellow revellers. They were not pictures of Alex as he had been seen in public, though – for he was dressed as a woman.

The uproar was immediate. Almost at once, the news became public (although, in truth, some people initially took this to be just another publicity stunt on Katie's part before realising that, yes, Alex was actually a cross-dresser), with Katie blithely talking about selling the pictures to a magazine. But Alex soon put a stop to all that: 'I'm a cage fighter – you can't do this!' he declared. And so Katie held back – for then.

Then a photo did actually surface: of Alex, sitting between two other men in drag, in full make-up and sporting a brunette wig. He was wearing a dark dress, offset with fetching scarlet nail varnish. People were stunned. Alex himself, meanwhile, was clearly not sure what to make of all the attention he was now receiving: should he go along with all this or point-blank deny it? The latter claim was increasingly less of an option, however, despite quite how much at odds the revelation was to his cage-fighting career.

'He is starting to realise how far Jordan will go to cash in on her fame,' remarked one of his friends. 'Those pictures would destroy his tough reputation.'

It began to emerge that his ex-girlfriend hadn't been joking when she said that Alex could be a little wild.

'Alex says, "I'm tri-sexual, I will try anything once" – I think that's a stupid comment on his behalf,' said another friend. 'But I am almost wanting him to hang himself a little bit and realise that Katie has got nothing but her own interests at heart – and that he needs to start having *his* own interests at heart.'

But facts were facts. 'I know it's something he's

done and been quite open about from the start, and that hasn't really fazed Kate at all,' said a source. 'The guy is an absolute animal when it comes to sex: he is a very sexual being. He just loves it constantly and it's a major thing he's always been into. I think there's a bit of a theme when it comes to it, and, whether that's male or female, I don't think he's that bothered.'

However, Katie and Alex remained lofty about it all, putting in an appearance at the Horse of the Year Show in Birmingham. That provoked a row with Pete: the couple left the children with their nanny and Katie's mother. 'Pete couldn't believe it when he found out that Katie had left the kids at home in Surrey while she spent the weekend in Birmingham,' said a friend. 'What she did went completely against what they'd agreed. He was furious. But it really upset him too, as he would have had no problem looking after them. He doesn't want anything like this to ever happen again.'

Another friend leaped to Katie's defence. 'Katie made sure she spent some quality time with all three children before she left to go to the show,' she protested. 'She attended Junior's Harvest Festival on Friday morning. Pete was invited, but decided not to go. She then went home and spent a couple of hours hanging out with Princess before setting off at 3pm.

She left the children in the care of their nanny and her mum, Amy.

'Katie recently installed CCTV cameras all over her house so that, when she's not at home, she can check on the kids. She had her laptop with her while she was in Birmingham and constantly logged on to see what the kids were doing.'

It seemed there was no sign of the tensions between the couple calming down any time soon.

But everyone's attention was still elsewhere. Alex's other vocal ex-girlfriend, Danielle Sims, also had something to contribute and explained that, yes, the allegations were all true. 'I went to his parents' place and his mum told me he was in his room,' she said. 'I went up, opened the door and found him sat on the bed dressed as a woman. I didn't say anything; I just looked and looked. I thought, Why are you wearing women's clothes? It didn't change my feelings towards him, but it made me feel a bit inadequate.'

Did it make her wonder whether Alex might gay, although, in fact, most cross-dressers aren't?

'It crossed my mind, of course it did,' she admitted. 'And, looking back, I did ask him. But his dressing in women's clothes wasn't the reason we eventually split up. It wasn't embarrassing, and I'd much rather a man cross-dressed on me than cheated on me. Jordan says he is a cross-dresser – and he is. I am sure he is annoyed that it's come out.'

However, Alex confided in Danielle that he was more than a little concerned as to where the story might be heading. 'Katie is stitching me up,' he said to her. 'She told the papers I'm a cross-dresser to make me look like a freak. I'm sure she did it so, when she dumps me, people won't blame her.'

Katie, however, point-blank denied that she had any intention of finishing with him: indeed, she appeared to be taking it all rather well. 'We are still very much together,' she said rather icily. Alex's alter ego, as it transpired, was called Roxanne. 'Jordan is very laidback about the fact it's been revealed,' a source commented. 'She is always of the opinion that the truth will always come out and so it is better to be upfront with things. Alex is not ashamed in the slightest. On the contrary, he thinks the subject matter is totally misunderstood. He has been totally upfront and honest with Kate and she is cool with it.

'Kate is very open-minded sexually, and very little can shock her. They are really happy together and nothing can break the special bond they share. Kate is nothing if not loyal. She'll stick with him through thick and thin. Nothing fazes her.'

Indeed, she was positively revelling in it. She

bought a new dressage horse, which she called Jordan's Cross Dresser and went on BBC's *The Graham Norton Show* in October to chat about her new friend's hobby. 'Before Alex met me, he hadn't dressed up for a year,' she chirped. 'And when he told me, I was like, "Oh my God, I've got to dress you up!" So I dress him – the wigs, eyelashes, everything. And at first he was like, "This is a bit weird, I'm not used to a girl doing me up."'

Unlike Danielle, Marie hadn't taken the news so well. 'He always said he would stop being Roxanne to please Marie, but he couldn't say goodbye,' said a friend. 'It made him feel comfortable and he couldn't give her up.' But Alex had become increasingly concerned that Marie was thinking of spilling the beans. 'I've got nothing to be ashamed of,' he told a friend. 'It's almost a form of blackmail. I want people to know the truth, but on my terms. I won't let her twist things and make what I do sound seedy.'

In truth, he still seemed a little unsure about how to cope with the revelations, although he asserted that the relationship with Katie remained strong. 'We have an amazing connection,' he said. 'We just want to be a normal couple.'

Indeed, the disclosure that, like Katie and Jordan, Alex and Roxanne were two different people in the same body could only have brought them closer together.

'He is very clean-living and doesn't smoke, but,when he is Roxanne, he puffs away like a chimney,' said a friend. 'And Roxanne is brilliant when it comes to cooking and cleaning as well. She is always throwing dinner parties for her friends while wearing her best glad-rags and is totally at ease. Alex, on the other hand, is rubbish and not the best when it comes to domestic duties around the house.'

Alex, or rather, Roxanne, was also extremely coy about sex. 'Jordan may think this is a kinky sex thing, but nothing could be further from the truth,' the friend continued. 'Roxanne is a lady who doesn't sleep with just anyone. In fact, he doesn't have sex as her at all, only as Alex. He is much more happy having cosy girlie nights in, trying out his girlfriends' lippy and having a good gossip. Saying that, when he's out of character, he's the complete opposite and an animal in the bedroom. He is utterly insatiable and a hot lover. It really is a remarkable transformation.'

What with all the excitement in Katie's life, it was easy to forget the fact that Pete was beginning to think about some companionship, too. He hadn't commented on all the revelations about Alex – yet – but did decide that it was finally time to look for a new love. 'I feel ready to meet someone else now,' pointedly adding, 'I am frustrated, but, whatever happens, I'm not going to throw it in front of the kids' faces. I'd like to meet someone, but I wouldn't want to show intimacy for a while in front of the kids. There has to come a point and I have to be careful, but I still want to move on. I've got three kids and some girl has to be willing to take that on. I'm not going to rush into marriage or anything. I'm not in a rush, but I am ready.'

Asked about rumours that he was dating Alesha Dixon, or, indeed, his nanny, he protested, 'I don't even have her phone number or use Facebook. I thought my nanny wanted to quit after the first day working with me when there was a story saying we were dating. My advice [to anyone in the same situation] is to fight for time with your kids. It's painful not being with them, but fight for all the time you can get.'

There had been suggestions (not least from Katie) that it wasn't good for the children to be constantly paraded on reality TV, but Pete was keen to defend his decision, too. 'You have to take the work, and, if you don't, what would I do?' he asked. 'There's loads of time to be with the kids off-screen, but, if I take the work, I think I'm buying a house for their future. It's such a small amount of time and we do so much when the cameras aren't there: they're fine.'

Yet another nasty incident between all the parties involved in the drama occurred, however. Pete became angry when he rang Katie to agree on a time to collect the kids, only for Katie to hand the phone over to Alex. And she lost no time in making clear what happened next by putting the details on Facebook: 'Pete said, "I'm gonna break your fucking legs – watch your back." Alex is a gentle guy, and Pete is not the sweet guy he always portrays. His true colours are starting to come out, thank God.'

Not that Alex wasn't capable of standing up for himself and he accused Pete of disrespect, adding, 'I'm the man of the house now.'

In an attempt to explain all, Pete went on *This Morning*. 'What really annoys me is when something private happens, within a minute, it's out there,' he said. 'The bottom line is, for five days, I was not allowed to speak to my kids. Anyone close to me knows that I couldn't speak to them, and then the night before last I got on the phone saying, "I want to speak to my kids," and I was handed the phone to this man, who said he's the man of the house now and he refused me to speak to my children.

'Now, I'm not perfect – I am human, I am a father and

I don't know any father that would not react to some man saying, "No, you're not speaking to them," and I lost my temper. I admit it. I'm tired of it – I just want to move on in every sense of the word. The kids are my life, I don't care about anything else but them – I've said that a million times, and everyone knows the only way to push my buttons is not to let me speak to my kids or see them, and that's what's been happening.'

It must be said, Alex had been a little tactless, admitting a few days previously, 'Junior did actually once call me "Dad". Of course, I corrected him immediately. I said, "No, I'm not Daddy, I'm Alex." As much as I'd love to be his father, he has a dad. Pete is good with them, I would never dispute his skills as a father.'

No one was disputing this either. What many were still wondering was Alex's suitability in a father's role. Further details of his more adventurous side were emerging, including an occasion when he got chummy with a ladyboy in Thailand without knowing it, and, when the realisation eventually dawned, he was not particularly alarmed.

'He was, like, "Oh, how funny!"' revealed a friend. 'He certainly didn't fly into a rage. The lads gave him some stick about it, but his attitude was, "It's all good fun, why beat yourself up about it?"'

Why indeed? 'They all went to a ladyboy bar, as you do – just to have a look and a laugh,' continued the friend. 'Alex was snogging a bird and he's then gone for a feel, but he got a lot more than he bargained for.'

And so had everyone else involved in the saga to date. Although Pete was watching the proceedings with slack-jawed amazement, he had not, as yet, said anything about Alex's little hobby. What's more, he would have been careful about saying too much – he didn't want to come across as being against cross-dressing.

But Pete would hardly have been human had he not allowed himself a frisson of concern, because the stories coming out now were getting increasingly sordid. Nor had Katie helped when she told Graham Norton that her sex life had never been so adventurous before. Of course, it was hardly surprising when Pete finally snapped – and he was about to do so very soon, too.

CHAPTER FIFTEEN

It's Over

In the wake of the revelations about Alex's interesting lifestyle, life refused to calm down – in fact, quite the opposite. Katie flew into a jealous rage when she saw pictures of Pete having dinner with Melanie Brown, aka Mel B, with whom he'd had a brief affair years earlier, despite the fact that Mel's husband, music producer Stephen Belafonte, was also present.

She was said to have sent him a text. 'You're welcome to her, Pete – go running back to all your exes.' It was an overreaction, all right, but also an indication of Katie's insecure state of mind.

The war continued on other fronts. In a poll of Best Celebrity Parents for Sky 1, Katie came near the bottom of the mothers' list, gaining just 2 per cent of the vote, while Pete came in at the top of the fathers', with 29 per cent of the vote, ahead of entries two and three – David Beckham and Brad Pitt. But then again, another poll – Bounty Celebrity Mum of the Year – put Katie on its shortlist, alongside Samantha Cameron, Mel B, Emma Bunton and Geri Halliwell.

There were also ongoing repercussions from Katie's appearance on *The Graham Norton Show* when she insinuated Pete was having an affair. This time, Pete threatened legal action and the offending sequence was cut.

'Graham said men were lazy and would "sleep with the first woman they see" and Katie agreed with him,' said a member of the audience. 'She said, "Yes" and then blurted out the name of the woman she believes Peter has slept with since they split up. The audience was stunned and so was Graham. It was like there was tumbleweed blowing through the studio. The BBC lawyers were already twitchy and they demanded the accusation be withdrawn from the show that will be screened.'

Katie also angered Pete by claiming he wanted a share of her fortune, something else the lawyers might be looking into. 'It looks like Pete's still after my money,' she told Graham. 'I texted him and said,

"Are you sticking to the pre-nup or are you after my money?"'

But why, asked Graham, didn't she talk to him directly about this?

'He won't talk to me – I've only seen him once since we split,' Katie replied.

In a separate interview, Katie stated, 'The trouble is, before, I felt married to two people – Pete and our management,' she said. 'And it was like Pete was married to two women – Claire and me. And it just suffocated me. If I'm going to blame anyone for the end of my relationship with Pete, I'd have to lay some of the blame with Claire.'

Claire had, of course, also been Katie's manager until the previous May, and she wasn't impressed with this version of events, either. 'Yes, I did have to control Kate to a certain extent, as can be seen since she stopped being my client,' she said. 'Pete doesn't need to be controlled like Kate, none of my other clients do – it was only her.'

In fact, Pete was becoming so exasperated that he issued a formal statement to 'put the record straight regarding the outrageous claims and lies'.

'I wish to make it perfectly clear for the record that my manager, Claire Powell, who I have known for the past 16 years, is my manager and a personal friend,' he said. 'She has never betrayed me or done anything other than support me, which is more than can be said for my ex-wife. I have said once before that if anybody slanders my name I will not hesitate in taking legal action and that is exactly what both Claire and I will do.'

But Katie didn't seem too deterred. She had a new book out, a guide to style called *Standing Out* and had promised the 'stunt to end all stunts' for the launch. Indeed, she was as good as her word. Katie's near-genius when it comes to self-promotion was at the fore yet again: she dressed up in a red gown and blonde Marilyn Monroe wig, and posed with four men (all dressed in drag, including Alex himself), sporting the gold lamé number Katie had worn in Ibiza. The other men, who were not commonly known as cross-dressers, were Katie's brother Danny Price, sporting a pink number from Katie's equestrian range, Andrew Gould – the horse trainer Pete was said to be jealous of – and Katie's close friend Phil Turner. It was meant to generate a huge amount of publicity, and so it did.

Alex, meanwhile, had clearly decided that, now everything was so much out in the open, he might as well go with the flow – and he did. 'It's a bit of fun – I've dressed up as a woman, and it's a laugh,' he said.

'If I go out and wear a dress, so fucking what? I bet loads of people who slag me off are secretly harbouring some desire that they're too scared to admit or experience. I'm very gay! I love the world! I'm tri-sexual, I'll try anything... I am just a man who is in love with his girlfriend.'

And finally, the decree absolute came in. Katie marked the occasion by giving an interview on *This Morning*, in which she implied the marriage had been little more than a business deal. 'Well, for me and Pete, it is a business – we all know the entertainment business is a fake world, not a real world.'

Pete begged to differ. 'This has been the most heartbreaking year of my life,' he said. 'For her to think it was a business deal just sums her up.'

Katie also made one last-ditch attempt to get Pete to talk to her. 'All I want to do is meet up with Pete,' she said. 'All I'd like to say to Pete is, "Let's just sit in a room, just us." I just don't hold anything against him. Let's be adults. At the end of the day, I have to keep ringing solicitors to discuss the children. I just want to ring Pete.'

But Pete, fearing whatever went on between them would immediately be made public, simply would not agree.

Phillip Schofield, who presents *This Morning*, had

known the couple for some time and wrote his take on it all on his blog. 'What makes this break-up even more upsetting is that they are communicating, but in the papers!' he said. 'Not really a reliable way to pick through the wreckage of a marriage. It's hard to know who is in the right and if what we are hearing is anywhere near the truth. I don't intend to take sides, I like them both, but this public scrap is anything but helpful. Katie also said on *This Morning* that she was running a business – well, if that's how we are to view it, then I'm beginning to feel more than a whiff of public boredom. With a couple who thrive off public interest, apathy must be the greatest danger. We want them both to be happy, but we admire dignity and restraint, which could be lacking in some quarters. This should not be about point-scoring, it should be about sensible adults behaving in a dignified way, if only for the sake of the children.'

While he might have been right about the wisdom of behaving with some restraint, he certainly wasn't correct when it came to public apathy. The public was lapping it up. As the divorce was finalised, Pete was pictured embracing his brother Michael and Claire. 'It's over,' he told them. 'I've moved on. It's been hard, but you guys have always been there for me. I've been hurt by this, but I'm a stronger man now. I can cope with anything.' He then went off to spend a day with his children.

And now, at long last, Pete really was free to find love again. 'He's a hot-blooded man and the last few months have been difficult,' said a source. 'But he's always wanted to do the right thing by Kate and the kids. And that meant not being on the market until things died down. Now that moment has finally come, expect some fireworks. Pete was always 100 per cent faithful during their marriage and even when the divorce was going through. You haven't seen Pete on the town legless and pulling people. He's been a model of restraint. He'll have a relaxing night in, looking after the kids. He might have a glass of Scotch when the kids go to bed.'

Chantelle Houghton, one of the many women Katie erroneously linked to her ex-husband, made a re-appearance: bizarrely, she was spotted hand-in-hand with Dane Bowers, another of Katie's exes. It was a small world.

The extent of Pete's popularity, and the admiration for the manner in which he handled the split, became apparent when he was asked to perform at a Christmas ball for the wives of British soldiers serving in Afghanistan.

'It's a real honour,' said Pete's manager Claire. 'Pete

was absolutely tickled that the wives specifically asked the corporals for him. It was decided something special should be put on for the wives because they have a difficult job, just like the guys out on the battlefield in Afghanistan. Every night when they put their children to bed, they have to tell their kids Daddy is OK, although they never truly know if their other half is safe. They're experts at putting on a brave face. Pete is touched at their request and can't wait to sing at the ball.'

Pete also finally addressed the issue of Alex's cross-dressing. It was a difficult subject to broach, because he obviously didn't want to come across as a bigot, but, like any father, he was understandably concerned about the impact it would have on his children. In the event, his tone was measured and his request reasonable – please don't do it when the kids are about.

'Whatever people are doing in their private lives, and that goes for them or anyone, can you please not do it in front of the kids,' he said. 'I'm not going to criticise, I'm not going to say, "How dare you do this or that" – just don't do it in front of the kids! Give me that little bit of respect.'

Quite how bitter the split had become came through from a different (and unexpected) quarter –

Michelle Clack. Not only had she been one of Katie's closest friends, but she had even been a bridesmaid at the wedding, and so, when she began to sound off, it was clear that, behind the scenes, something really had gone very wrong. And her attack, when it came, was both devastating and vicious.

'She is a nasty, selfish bitch and a shameless liar who needs serious therapy,' said Michelle, in an interview with the *News of the World*. 'She is spiralling out of control and it's getting worse. The Jordan alter ego is the more powerful force in her life again than Katie Price. Seeing the monster unleashed is scary. Jordan was my best friend, but I can't stand by and watch how she's treated Pete. After everything she's been saying, I believe the truth about their marriage has to come out.'

Like Katie, Michelle was a glamour model (in fact, Katie inspired her first breast enhancement) and she had known her for years and never spoken openly about her before, which gave the attack even more force. 'Me and Kate have shared many beds,' she said. 'We've seen each other naked many times. There's nothing to hide between us. In 15 years, we had never had an argument or exchanged bad words, but, 18 months ago, her personality started to change. Even though Kate has built her reputation on sex and being sexy, it's all an act for work. She doesn't actually like sex and will usually do anything she can to avoid having it.

'Over the last two years, their relationship had become almost entirely sexless. Her excuse would always be that she was working hard and had three kids. She'd always say to me, "Oh no, I'm always too tired, I can't be bothered." But it didn't sit right with Pete because this all happened at the same time she started to go out on the town much more and dress up very sexily. Jordan was back. Kate uses sex to get things she needs. When she first met Pete, she said her sex life was awesome – just what she's saying at the moment about her new boyfriend, Alex Reid.'

Michelle's husband, Nick Baker, was a close friend of Pete's. 'I remember having conversations with Pete, where the subject of sex would come up,' he said. 'He'd say, "I don't know anything about it, I haven't had it for so long. Does she even fancy me?" She was portrayed as a sex symbol, spoke about sex all the time on TV and in magazines, but wasn't putting out to her husband.'

And that wasn't all. 'Kate always made it clear the house in Woldingham was hers,' said Michelle. 'Peter wanted to buy half with Kate, but she never let him. He made sure he went halves on everything, from the cinema to furniture to bills. But when he wanted to make any changes, she'd say, "What are you saying? This is my house." She hated the thought of him being more successful than her, so found ways to make him feel terrible.

'Kate's mum Amy always made Pete feel inferior, too. When he'd been working all day in the recording studio in the garden, which he had paid to restore, she would make pointed comments like, "Oh, so you're not working today?" Neither Katie nor Amy believed he'd have any success with his music and were openly scornful of it. Kate would always refuse to listen to his songs and she'd be annoyed when Peter spoke to visitors to the house about them. She'd say, "Nobody's interested."'

If there was even a grain of truth in all of this, it was a miracle that the marriage lasted as long as it did. But Katie did still have one staunch defender: her mother Amy, who also got a mention in dispatches, courtesy of Michelle, and who came out fighting for her daughter.

'I'm so angry and somebody has to start sticking up for Kate,' she said. 'As much as I don't want to say anything, people have to hear the truth. I was with Kate when she was having the miscarriage and the doctor said, "I'm sorry, Kate, it's not there. It's not forming. It's dead. There's no heartbeat." It was so upsetting. But, as far as Pete was concerned, he was like, "Come on, it's happened. You have to move on."

'You could see that when they filmed the London Marathon immediately afterwards for ITV, he didn't seem to give two shits about her. He was asking why she was upset and things like, "Why are you so moody?" when he knew what had gone on, just days before. I thought it was insensitive and his reaction surprised her. She was so upset and couldn't stop crying.'

As for his music, Amy said that she was a little surprised by the recent album. 'It was about failing relationships and he was continually running her down,' she mused. 'I thought, Maybe this was what songwriters did, but then I thought, Hang on, how could he do that? They were still married and it was just wrong, not normal. It was almost as if the last year was all pre-planned and little more than a sham.'

Nor, said Amy, was Pete half as easy-going as he appeared. 'He's a great actor and can turn it on and off,' she said. 'When filming was on, he was always quite bubbly, but I have seen Peter when he's on one of his lows, especially when he's manipulative, moody and verbally aggressive. One day he was rowing with Kate while she had post-natal depression and I left to go home but I was a bit worried. She was vulnerable and he was laying into her – not physically, but verbally – and I had to go back to make sure she was all right. Maybe I was overreacting, but I was just worried. Pete didn't seem to understand what she was going through.'

And as far as their sex life went – 'She lost the baby just before the London Marathon, so they must have been at it then,' continued Amy. 'Princess is just over two, so she was obviously doing it then. How does Michelle know intimate parts of their marriage? If Kate wasn't having sex, it was because she was working hard and had lots of pressure, like any working parent. It's a sad thing because it's the end of what they both wanted, but the fact it's being played out in the public eye is the most distressing thing. The mudslinging has got so bad that it has to stop. The only people benefiting are the lawyers. All they need to do is pick up the phone – but he's refusing to talk to her, so it's hopeless.'

But Pete refused to comment. Writing in *New! Magazine*, however, he did relate how the sight of Alex playing with his children brought on a panic attack, something he had suffered when he was much younger, but had thought was over. 'I honestly haven't had anything happen like this for years, but it occurred on the same day that I saw the first pictures of Alex Reid with my children and it really set me back,' he said. 'I found it unbelievably hard to see another man with Junior and Princess, and that was probably the lowest I've felt throughout the whole split.

'It's any father's nightmare to see pictures like that and I went to bed feeling not only heartbroken, but also massively anxious, which obviously brought on the attack. I've always said that the only things that got to me are anything to do with the children and it's the truth.

'It happened about three months ago and it's all a bit of a blur. I knew what was happening, so I got up with the intention of getting my brother, Mike. I felt so anxious that I wanted him to take me to hospital, but I didn't make it out of my bedroom and all I remember is hearing a bang. The next thing I knew, I woke up on the floor. I lay there for about half an hour in a daze and then I noticed there was a line of blood trickling down the wall of my bedroom where I'd hit my head after losing consciousness.'

Katie, meanwhile, was livid about Michelle's interview and proceeded to hit back in the only way she knew how – by implying that she and Pete were having an affair. 'One of my friends chose not to see me any more after me and Peter split,' she said, knowing this would be particularly hurtful given Pete was friends with Michelle's husband. 'I was really upset at the time and now I hear she's seeing Pete. If that's the case, then his girlfriend is one of my ex-friends, which I predicted would happen. I hope he does have a girlfriend and I wouldn't be surprised if it's her.'

Pete issued a denial, which was almost unnecessary, given this was so clearly untrue. Writing in *New!* magazine, he said: 'Another week, another pack of lies from Kate,' he said. 'This week, she has been saying there were three people in our marriage. I would like to say it's absolutely not true … Claire is engaged to her long-term partner Neville and has a child with him, and we've worked together for 16 years and never been anything more than friends. It's ironic Katie keeps accusing me of sleeping with all these people when she's the one who has a new boyfriend.'

Of course, but for how long? Shortly after Pete wrote this, there were reports that Alex had left Katie's home and moved back in with his mother following a series of rows. 'I hope we can stay together,' Alex told a friend. 'But, if not, I've had a good run.'

It was no coincidence that this happened

immediately after the divorce was finalised. That was it now – the marriage really was over, and, whatever bravado she displayed in public, Katie was devastated. 'She's been crying hysterically, on and off all week,' said a source. 'When the divorce was finalised, it really hit her hard. She may come across as having a tough exterior, but she's broken by the split with Pete and she's trying to persuade herself that being with Alex is what she needs.

'She's been distant and acting weird with him all week. Alex was trying to comfort her, but, every time he tried to cuddle her, she'd snap, "Get away from me!" He yelled back, "You're clearly not over Pete!" She told him it would be best if he gave her a few days' space. He agreed and left, although he's hoping they can hold things together.'

One problem seemed to be that Alex felt a little overexposed, especially after posing with Katie at her book launch. His little secret certainly wasn't a private thing any more, and, for all that the world is a more tolerant place than it once was, cage fighting and cross-dressing are not the most obvious bedmates: Alex had been set up for a lot of future stick.

'He's finally realising that she's all about one person – herself,' revealed a source. 'He does love her, but the cross-dressing issue became the real problem. Her being so open and brazen about it left him feeling humiliated. Katie's mum, Amy, and brother Danny are very worried about her. She comes across super-strong, but behind closed doors she's a different character on the brink.'

Increasingly, it was looking as if Pete's way of coping was ultimately the more sensible one. He had sat down, grieved, come to terms with what had happened and was now beginning to think about dating again. Katie, on the other hand, had been so determined to put on a show of public defiance that she simply hadn't allowed herself time to work through it all. Now it was catching up with her and she didn't know what to do.

'She just can't let go of Pete,' continued the source. 'Everything she does comes back to Pete – she can't stop talking about him. She needs to move on for her own sake. One thing they have agreed on is that they would not leave the children with a nanny, if the other one was free to look after them. Katie's broken this agreement and that will be another thing that will rile Pete.'

Indeed, everything seemed to rile Pete – but then everything riled Katie, too. And it was hard to escape the impression that, if she couldn't have Pete back, which is clearly what she wanted, then she would do everything in her power to annoy him, whether it was accusing him of having affairs or flaunting new men in front of him. And, while Pete might have wanted Katie to leave him alone, the fact that they had children together meant that simply couldn't happen. They were – and are – bound together: neither will ever be free.

It's all a long way from the jungle and the romance that first began in 2004, culminating in the fairytale wedding, two years later. Katie dressed as a princess for the occasion in a pink tulle skirt and a tiara, while Pete was her handsome prince. She rode in a glass carriage to the nuptials: it was a fairytale come to life. Now, if it remained a fairytale, then it was like something written by the Brothers Grimm, with a couple locked in a never-ending battle, in which no one could ever be the winner, where there could only be two opposing sides.

Team Kate or Team Pete? So, who would ultimately come out on top?